A GUIDE
TO THE
PASSION

100 Questions about
THE PASSION OF THE CHRIST

By the editors of Catholic Exchange

ASCENSION PRESS
West Chester, PA

Catholic Exchange
Your Faith • Your Life • Your World
Encinitas, CA

I have concluded that the materials presented
in this work are free of doctrinal or moral errors.

Nihil obstat: Bernadeane Carr, STL
                    Censor Librorum
                    March 2, 2004

In accord with 1983 CIC 827 § 3, permission to
publish this work is hereby granted.

Imprimatur: +Robert H. Brom
                  Bishop of San Diego
                  March 2, 2004

For permission to reproduce the materials contained herein, please contact
the publisher at info@ascensionpress.com or at the address below.

Ascension Press
Post Office Box 1990
West Chester, PA 19380
Orders: (888) 488-6789
www.AscensionPress.com

Cover design: Kinsey Caruth

Printed in the United States of America

ISBN 1-932645-42-X

Contents

Introduction

By now you have most likely seen the stunning film, *The Passion of The Christ*. It is my hope that it touched your heart as it did mine and piqued your interest in learning more about the very familiar but often misunderstood story of Jesus' suffering, death, and triumph over the grave.

The release of this movie comes some ten years into my own personal re-conversion to the Catholic faith of my upbringing. Experiencing this film has not only reaffirmed my faith but has also moved me to share what I've come to know as a Catholic who discovered the treasures of our Faith for the first time after a long period of wandering in the desert. My hope is that you might have a more direct path to the full appreciation and faithful practice of the Gospel than I did.

This film arrives not a moment too soon given our ever-deteriorating entertainment culture and its tendency to distract us from serious consideration of the Great Questions—*Who am I?*, *How did I get here?*, *What must I do?* and *Where am I going?* Jesus has been placed directly in front of us by one of our most respected filmmakers and we are compelled to take notice and decide where we stand on the question of Christ. The question He asked Simon Peter 2,000 years ago is the question He still asks us: "Who do you say I am?"

As someone involved in the distribution and marketing of the film, I noticed early on the fervor with which many Protestant communities were preparing to use the film for evangelistic purposes. Websites sprang up featuring downloadable materials about Jesus and the gospels. Marketing companies began churning out posters and flyers promoting the film and their own faith communities. Tracts poured into circulation making the case for Christ as the key to peace and happiness in life.

In terms of effecting conversions and motivating people to weed out sin from their lives—which is what meditating on the Passion of Christ is all about—our evangelical brothers and sisters have been an inspiration. But can their theology adequately mine such cinematic gems as the Last Supper flashbacks or the deeply Marian themes presented in the movie? Though the founders of some of the prominent Protestant denominations believed in Christ's real presence in the Eucharist, this fact has been lost today in huge portions of American Protestantism. And without an understanding of Mary as our model in true Christian faith, one cannot begin to understand her significant role in the film. Only the fullness of Catholic faith can help us grasp these essential elements that figure so prominently in the Scriptural record, the apostolic Tradition, and the film.

The Passion of The Christ quite poignantly links the sacrifice of the cross with the Eucharistic sacrifice of the Mass. In doing so, it faithfully depicts biblical and Catholic teaching. Yet the Eucharistic connections between the Passion and the Mass are not obvious to many Catholics today. Indeed, speaking out of my own experience as a clueless Catholic ten years ago, I can only say that it's highly unlikely that such connections are obvious even to those who have been born and raised in the Church. This is not because the connections are not there, but because so many people have not received an education in the Faith that equips them to *see* those connections, which are quite real and are, in fact, delineated for us in the teaching of the Church. Therefore, we at *CatholicExchange.com* see a need for this book to provide answers to some of the many questions critical to a full understanding of authentic Christianity—questions *The Passion of The Christ* will most certainly raise.

Everyone has an awareness of God and His still, small voice on some level. It is in how we respond to the voice that we define to what degree we are truly Christian. We are often just one tragedy or one near-miss away from being shaken into a keen and urgent awareness of God and what He has created and called us to be. May this movie and a careful study of its meaning and relevance take the place of that misfortune and set us in a direction of positive change and authentic conversion. May it set us on a path toward recognizing and pursuing the specific mission God has ordained for us from the beginning of time. And may we receive the grace we need to accomplish it.

The Passion of The Christ is a sign of contradiction in our time. May your viewing of it be the divine surprise that sets you on course and may this book be the key that helps unlock its deeper meaning and unleash the full power of Christ in your life.

—Tom Allen
Editor and President,
CatholicExchange.com
February 10, 2004

PART I
100 QUESTIONS AND ANSWERS

1) **What does the word "Passion" mean in relation to this film?**

   "Passion" means "agony" or "suffering." The "Passion of Christ" is generally understood to begin with the final meal Jesus had with His twelve apostles (the Last Supper); it continues through His agony and betrayal in the Garden of Gethsemane, His trial before Pontius Pilate, His scourging at the pillar, His carrying of the cross, and ends with His crucifixion and death. The film covers only these final hours in the life of Jesus.

2) **Where does the opening scene of the movie take place?**

   In the Garden of Gethsemane, which is located just outside the city gates of Jerusalem at the foot of the Mount of Olives. There are several olive trees in this garden today that are more than 3,000 years old—so they existed in the time of Jesus, and may have been the actual trees under which He prayed. The Garden of Gethsemane is one of the most visited sites in the Holy Land.

3) **Christians refer to Jesus' "agony in the Garden." What does this phrase mean and what is its significance?**

   Christians understand Jesus' prayer in the Garden of Gethsemane to be one of intense spiritual, emotional, and even physical pain. The general belief is that Jesus, whom all Christians profess to be God Incarnate, understood the profound suffering—or agony—He would soon experience and, like any human, was tormented by the thought. He said to the three disciples with Him, "My soul is very sorrowful, even to death" and prayed to the Father, "if it be possible, let this cup pass from me; nevertheless, not as I will, but as You will" (Matthew 26:38, 39).

4)   What do the words "God Incarnate" mean in reference to Jesus?

Incarnate means "enfleshed." Christians believe that God, at a specific moment in time (about 4 BC), took on human flesh (not just a body, but also a soul). It was a real and complete human nature, not just a human appearance—not a mask or "costume." This is the mystery of the Incarnation, and the reason why Christians place such great emphasis on the celebration of Christmas and, increasingly, the Annunciation—the moment when God became man by being conceived in Mary's womb (see Luke 1:26-38).

5)   Before we go any further, is there any hard evidence that Jesus really existed and that the events portrayed in the movie actually took place?

Yes, there is much evidence that Jesus really existed and that the general events portrayed in the movie occurred in history. No serious historian, not even the most secular, doubts the existence of Jesus.

Various secular sources attest to Jesus' existence and corroborate many of the events described in the Bible. (For more information on this point, see the Resources section at the end of this book.) The primary source of evidence, though, is the Bible itself, the greatest and most carefully examined book in human history.

6) How can the New Testament be historically accurate when it talks about the Passion? Wasn't it written long after these events?

The earliest books in the New Testament (the part of the Bible about the life of Jesus and the beginning of the Church) were probably written less than twenty years after Jesus' death and resurrection. These are the letters of Paul and they are written to churches that have already heard the basic story of Jesus' Passion and Resurrection. The information in these letters reflects Paul's and his audience's shared awareness of the same data we find in the gospels (which had not yet been written).

Paul knows Jesus is a Jew of King David's line (Romans 1:3); that John the Baptist was His forerunner and had disavowed any claim to his own Messiahship (Acts 13:24-25); that His chief disciples were Peter, James, and John (Galatians 2: 9); that He had predicted His return "like a thief" (1 Thessalonians 5:4); that He had instituted the Eucharist (1 Corinthians 11:23-25); that He had been rejected by the Jewish leaders (1 Thessalonians 2:15), tried under Pontius Pilate (1 Timothy 6: 13) and crucified for us (Galatians 3:1); that He was laid in a tomb (Acts 13:29); that He had been raised from the dead and seen by many witnesses (1 Corinthians 15:3-8); and that He had ascended into heaven (Ephesians 4:9-10). How does Paul know all this? Much the same way you know about Ronald Reagan's presidency or about John Lennon: because twenty years isn't all that long and there are still lots of witnesses around whom Paul knows personally.

In fact, St. Paul, writing to the Church in Corinth, made it plain that there were more than 500 eyewitnesses to the Risen Christ and that the vast majority of them were still alive when he was writing (in the late 50s). And, of course, Paul himself had seen the Risen Christ.

The gospels were written just a bit later than Paul's letters—in the 60s and 70s. Three of them are the products of eyewitnesses of the events (Matthew, Mark, and John). Luke was written by a man who was a close companion of Paul and who had multiple opportunities to hear the testimony of people who were present for the events recorded in his gospel. Would you find it difficult to believe that somebody who was not present for the events, writing today, could possibly give an accurate account of the administration of President Kennedy, based on multiple written sources and interviews with eyewitnesses?

In short, the gospels are highly reliable accounts of the events of Christ's ministry, written quite close to the actual events. Moreover, they corroborate each other to a remarkable extent, while at the same time preserving just the sort of differences of emphasis one would expect in real eyewitness testimony.

7) So, in the Garden, Jesus knew He was going to die?

Yes. Since Jesus is the all-knowing God, He knew He was going to die. But, because He was fully man as well, He suffered terrible anguish anticipating the torture and death He was about to endure. You and I, as human beings, possess a human nature. Jesus, though, as God Incarnate, possessed two natures: human and divine. So, in His divine nature He knew things that only God could know; in His human nature He experienced everything as we do—except sin. He hungered, He thirsted, and He felt pain.

8) As an aside, why are you capitalizing the word "He" when referring to Jesus?

To show respect for Jesus as a divine Person—as God, Creator of the universe.

9) Did Jesus actually sweat blood during His agony?

According to Luke, that seems to be what happened: "He was in such agony and He prayed so fervently that His sweat became like drops of blood falling on the ground" (Luke 22:43-44). Such a phenomenon (known as *hematidrosis*) is not unknown to medical science, and similar things have been recorded of other people in moments of extreme mental, emotional, and physical stress. Jesus, in anguish over what He knew was about to happen, nonetheless prayed that His Father's will be done. But He was a real human being. Therefore, He experienced the weight of all the sins—past, present, and future—of the entire world, and the burden of these transgressions was so profound that He may well have sweat blood.

10) In the Garden of Gethsemane scene, shortly before the soldiers come to arrest him, we hear Jesus say the words, "Father, if it be possible, let this cup pass from Me." What does this mean?

In His humanity, Jesus was asking God the Father if He could avoid the cross He would soon embrace. The "cup" was the cup of bitter suffering and death. In fact, when people later argued that Jesus was not fully man, this text was brought forward to prove that He did have a human will; human beings naturally desire to avoid pain and death. Yet as God, Jesus knew that there was no turning back; there was no other way to reconcile fallen humanity with God. He had to assume a debt that mankind could never pay. As an act of supreme love, He would lay down His life for His friends—us. The Bible tells us that Jesus assented to this plan of redemption ("not as I will, but as You will") and that God the Father sent angels to console Him in His agony.

11) Why did God the Father require Jesus to take upon Himself such tremendous physical and emotional suffering?

God is not a harsh, overbearing Father who requires the suffering of his Son. Human beings freely created a wall between themselves and God through centuries of pride, disobedience, and selfishness beginning with Adam and Eve. Jesus *freely* came into the world to perform an act of such intense humility, obedience, and love, that it would obliterate the wall

(John 10:18). The forces of human sin and demonic fury collaborated to hurl at Jesus every possible punishment and torture to turn Him back from His mission. But in so doing, they unwittingly proved the perfection of His love and provided Jesus with the Cross, the very instrument of salvation.

12) The movie shows three other men with Jesus in the Garden. Who are they?

They are Peter, James, and John, the three most important apostles, based on the number of times they appear in the Bible and the number of key experiences they share with Jesus.

Peter was a fisherman by trade. Originally known as Simon, he was renamed "Rock" (*Kephas* in Aramaic, *Petros* in Greek) by Jesus. At the prompting of his brother, Andrew, and at Jesus' invitation, Peter became a follower of Christ. In Matthew 16:18, Jesus states that He will establish the Church on Peter, the "rock," giving him great authority. Catholics see in this act of Christ the establishment of Peter as head of the apostles, as the head of the Church—the first pope.

James and John were brothers, the sons of Zebedee. The Bible tells us that they too were fishermen. One of the four gospels, the Book of Revelation, and three of the New Testament letters bear John's name.

13) There is a fifth figure in the Garden, whom I later realized represented the devil. Why is the devil present in the Garden?

The devil is there to tempt Jesus. By putting the devil in the Garden, the director faithfully reflects the gospel of Luke. While the other three gospels present the devil as tempting Jesus only in the desert, Luke 4:13 says (following the temptations in the desert) the devil left off tempting Jesus "until an opportune time." Luke, who actually says more about the devil's activity than any of the other gospels, doesn't mention the devil again until the Last Supper, when the devil is described as influencing Judas. In Luke, Jesus also says "the reign of darkness" has come, when He is arrested. A reasonable conclusion therefore is that the "opportune time" for the devil to resume his tempting is the Passion.

14) The devil asks Jesus a question during this scene in the Garden, saying, "Do you really believe one man can bear the full burden of sin?" Did this actually happen?

This questioning by the devil does not appear in the Bible, so here we have an example of the filmmaker taking some creative license. Based on the other instances in the Scriptures where Jesus is tempted by the devil, however, it is entirely plausible that such an exchange could have occurred. The devil loves such "golden opportunities" to undermine our resolve when we are experiencing intense suffering.

15) As the film's opening line of dialogue between Christ and the devil, am I to assume that this question about "the burden of sin" is foundational to the entire plot?

Yes, this exchange actually establishes the whole premise of the movie—the very meaning of Jesus' suffering and death, which, as God, He had the power to avoid. Jesus would offer Himself as the spotless (i.e., sinless) Lamb to be sacrificed for the atonement of the sins of humanity.

16) But why did Jesus have to die?

As we have noted, death is the just consequence of our sin, because in sinning, we turn our backs on God, the Source of our life. Jesus took the consequences of our sin—death—in our place.

As horrific as Jesus' death was, we need to appreciate a fundamental truth of human existence: authentic love involves sacrifice. Love involves the total giving of self. Love can even mean "[laying] down one's life for one's friends" (John 15:13). So there is transcendent meaning in sacrifice and suffering. If endured for the good of others, it is truly sanctifying and salvific. To a world that tries to avoid discomfort of any sort, this seems ridiculous. Instead, it is just one of countless examples of how the way of Truth runs counter to human expectations. This, by the way, has always been the case. The first people to hear the story of Jesus were just as struck as we are today at the strangeness of it. St. Paul wrote 2,000 years ago, "For the word of the cross is folly to those who are perishing, but to us who are being saved it is the power of God" (1 Corinthians 1:18).

17) Couldn't God have chosen to simply declare humanity's relationship with Him restored? Why did He choose such an extreme and bloody means of reconciling the world to Himself?

In suffering, we actually come to understand more about God's unfathomable love. The idea that God reveals His love for us through the Passion and death of Christ is stated clearly in the Bible when Jesus (after His resurrection) reveals to His disciples: "Was it not necessary that the Christ should suffer these things and enter into His glory?" (Luke 24: 26). Why was suffering necessary? To restore to us what the original humans (Adam and Eve) had lost through disobedience. In their disobedience, they sinned against God's law and began to love themselves and other things more than they loved God—who should be first in every person's heart. They lost the privilege of life with God and when they lost it, they lost it for us as well.

Love involves self-giving, the sacrificing of our selfish desires for the good of another. After the Fall, human desires became self-seeking and disordered. Christ's redemption for us—His taking on of the burden of sin—not only restored our relationship with God, but also taught us the true meaning of love: sacrifice. In short, words are cheap. It is through actions that we prove our love. To understand suffering for love is to understand God. To understand God is to understand life.

18) Things are starting to connect for me now. Didn't the timing of the Christ's Passion have something to do with the Jewish Passover?

Yes, and this explains much. For those of you who are familiar with the Bible (or have seen the epic film, *The Ten Commandments*), you will remember that God called Moses to lead his people out of slavery in Egypt (see Exodus 3:4-10). This event, which occurred about 1,200 years before the birth of Jesus, is key to understanding Christ's Passion, because the Passion is the fulfillment of the Jewish Passover ritual.

As Scripture tells us, the night the Hebrews were set free from slavery in Egypt, God sent the angel of death to claim the first-born of every household. The Lord promised, however, that death would "pass over" His chosen people *if* they put the blood of a lamb on their doorposts; the blood would save them (see Exodus, chapters 11 and 12). After more than 1,000 years of the Jewish people commemorating this saving event of Passover, Jesus came as the ultimate Passover offering and revealed its full meaning: by the shedding of His blood—the blood of the spotless, sinless Lamb of God—sin and death are finally conquered; they no longer have power over us.

The Passover event of Exodus is a foreshadowing of Christ's death on the cross. The blood of Jesus, the perfect "Lamb," would be sprinkled on the cross (the doorpost) for His followers. All who accept Christ and keep His commandments will be saved by His blood; death "passes over" them, for they have eternal life. That is exactly why Jesus began His own Passion by celebrating the Passover with His disciples and transforming it into the Eucharist, the meal in which we now receive His Body under the form of bread and the cup of His Blood under the form of wine, which saves us from eternal death.

19) Is this the reason why there's so much blood in this movie?

Yes. The blood is key to understanding the sacrifice of the Lamb—Jesus, who took away the sin of the world. Just as blood is shed by soldiers who lay down their lives for their country or by mothers in childbirth, sacrificial love often involves the shedding of blood. It is no coincidence that the

Passion of Christ took place precisely at the time of the Jewish Passover. It is one of many fulfillments of Old Testament prophecy and is fundamental to understanding God's actions throughout history to save the human race.

20) Let's go back to the dialogue in the Garden between Jesus and the devil. The devil states that the price of saving people's souls would be too costly. What does he mean by these words?

This is merely the devil's futile attempt to dissuade Jesus from accepting the cross and fulfilling His mission. He was saying to Jesus that the amount of suffering He would endure would be too great a price to pay.

Having rejected God, the devil surely harbors immense hatred for the Creator. We also know from Scripture that he intends to wage spiritual battle against humans, God's special creation. We read in Genesis, "I will put enmity between you and the woman, and between your seed and her seed" (Genesis 3:15). This enmity includes desiring that humans lose their salvation. Thus he did what he could to try to discourage and prevent Jesus from accomplishing His saving mission.

21) The devil unleashes a snake in the Garden of Gethsemane and Jesus crushes it under His foot. What is the symbolism here?

Since this action is not mentioned in the Bible, it represents another instance of the director taking some artistic license for dramatic effect. However, the *symbolism* of Jesus' action *is* rooted in the

Scriptures. In the book of Genesis, God reveals that the "seed of the woman" (representing both mankind and, ultimately, Jesus, who is the "Son of Man" and representative of all humanity) will "bruise the head" of the serpent (Genesis 3:15). Jesus is the "new Adam" (see 1 Corinthians 15:22), restoring what the first Adam had lost through sin. So Jesus' crushing of the serpent in this scene is used here as a foreshadowing of Christ's victory over the devil and over sin and death through His suffering, death, and resurrection.

22) Is the devil character in the film meant to represent an actual spiritual being or is he merely symbolic of the "evil" in the world?

Far from being some abstract personification of "evil," the devil is an actual spiritual being—a fallen angel (or demon). Though this idea sounds quaint or old-fashioned to modern ears, the Catholic Church has consistently taught that the devil is a real being with formidable will and intellect. Being a pure spirit, he is not subject to the laws of the physical world. His natural intellectual abilities far surpass those of human beings. Both the Bible and the Tradition of the Church teach that the devil (also called Satan—meaning "adversary," or Lucifer—"light bearer") was the most glorious of the angels, but pride and envy caused him and his followers to rebel against God. As a result of this rebellion, Satan and the other fallen angels (or demons) were cast from God's presence, a separation that will exist for all eternity.

Given the devil's rejection of God, we can reason that he is consumed with hatred towards God and those made in God's image and likeness—humans. Satan, therefore, is surely relentless in his desire to have you and me lose our souls and be separated eternally from the God who loves us. In the movie, and particularly in the scene in the Garden, his aim is to derail Christ's mission on earth—a mission of love, truth, and salvation.

23) I have heard people, including some Christian teachers, explain that Satan is not real.

Believing in the devil may seem passé to the supposedly "enlightened," but this is a grave mistake. As C.S. Lewis points out in *The Screwtape Letters*, the widespread disbelief in Satan's existence is actually an ingenious move on the part of the Evil One. If he can convince men that he does not exist— that he is as "real" as the boogeyman—then we will not be on guard against him. And if we're not on guard against him, we will almost certainly fall into his traps. Because the reality is that he desperately wants your soul.

Jesus refers to the devil many times in Scripture. For example, in Matthew 25:41, He condemns those who refuse to follow His will and love their neighbor with the words, "Depart from me, you cursed, into the eternal fire prepared for the devil and his angels." In these words, Jesus joins the fate of those who refuse to do His will with that of the devil— namely, hell. The apostle John makes the essential mission of Jesus clear in his first letter: "The reason the Son of God appeared was to destroy the works of the devil" (1 John 3:8).

24) While we're on the subject of the devil, please define "sin" for me.

Sin is any free, deliberate behavior on our part that we know offends God and breaks His law.

25) Why is sin such a big deal?

First of all because God, as our creator and loving Father, deserves all of our love, respect, and obedience. But He really does not need our obedience—we do. For He loves us more than we love ourselves and knows us better than we know ourselves. So every time we say "no" to Him and His will, we damage ourselves and others. Some sin, called venial or light, weakens our relationship with God. Mortal or deadly sin ruptures our relationship with Him. This relationship is restored by turning away from sin and seeking His grace.

26) Why is there so much sin and opposition to God?

Because of the sin of our first parents (*original sin*), we inherit a humanity that has a natural tendency towards sin. But that is not the whole story. Satan is a master at deceitful advertising. He makes sin appear glamorous and desirable, just as he did in the Garden of Eden (Genesis 3). He tries to convince us that God forbids things not because they are harmful, but because they will make us like Him and He wants to keep us down, subservient, under His feet. So Satan markets sin as liberating while it is the exact opposite—enslaving. Our first parents fell for it, and so do we.

People's sins are rooted in their pride, anger, envy, greed, lust, gluttony, and laziness, otherwise known as the "seven deadly sins." Whereas choosing the high road can be difficult, choosing the evils of this world can be very attractive at times. It can all be traced back to the fall of Lucifer, the "Angel of Light"—the devil—who rebelled against God and established his kingdom on earth. God thereafter has allowed people the freedom to choose for themselves between His way of truth, selflessness, and light, and the devil's way of lies, selfishness, and darkness.

27) If sin is such a grave matter, why don't we hear more about it in the public discourse?

We live today in a permissive society that embraces sin as virtue. There are the ways of God and there are the ways of the world—two very different ways for humanity to live. The communications media is often filled with the implicit message that "anything goes" and that sin is "no big deal."

28) I realized later that the person who kisses Jesus in the Garden is Judas, one of the apostles. Why did he betray Jesus?

Besides being motivated by money (see John 12:6), Judas seems to have expected Jesus to be a different kind of messiah, a worldly one who would free Israel from the bondage of its Roman oppressors. Having witnessed Jesus' miracles, it is possible that Judas believed in Jesus' divinity, or at least grasped that He was a prophet. It is sometimes thought that Judas turned Jesus over to the authorities to force His hand—to cause Jesus to exercise His authority and restore the Jewish nation to earthly glory.

29) Who was Judas?

Actually, Scripture tells us little about him besides his name (Judas Iscariot) and his role as the apostles' treasurer. After betraying Jesus, he was seized with remorse and committed suicide by hanging himself.

"Iscariot" means "dagger," which is an interesting name in light of his role in betraying Jesus—"stabbing Him in the back," as the saying goes. It is also believed that his family hailed from the town of Kerioth in the south of Judea.

From the parts of the Bible that mention Judas we can create some sort of psychological profile of him. He seemed to be very concerned with "earthly" things, such as power and money. He rebuked Mary of Bethany who used expensive oil to anoint Jesus' feet. Judas griped that the money should be used for the poor. Judas also served as treasurer for the disciples, and the Bible says that he stole contributions from the money bag (John 12:6).

Judas seems to have felt remorse for his betrayal of Jesus because, as we see later in the film, he throws the thirty pieces of silver he was paid to betray Jesus on the floor of the Temple (see Matthew 27:5). He even says to the priests and scribes with whom he collaborated, "I have sinned in betraying innocent blood" (Matthew 27:4). This shows that Judas wasn't totally without conscience. Even so, this remorse was not followed by the virtue of hope—a hope that he could be forgiven. The Bible reveals that after he cast the thirty pieces of silver on the Temple floor he went out and hanged himself (see Matthew 27:5). He could have become a great saint had he recovered from his sin as Peter did. Instead, he despaired of God's mercy and chose death.

30) A fight scene in the Garden between the Temple guards and Jesus' disciples follows Judas' betrayal of Jesus. Peter cuts off the ear of one of the guards with his sword, and the guard is entranced by the way Jesus heals him. Did this actually happen?

The Bible tells us about the fight, the injury, and Jesus' healing (see Matthew 26:51 and Luke 22:51). It does not, however, mention anything about the spiritual odyssey the injured guard seems to go through.

While this addition in the film represents artistic license, it is a very logical one: Such a fight would be fast and furious. Imagine that you are the Temple guardsman. You feel the sharp pain of the sword slice through your ear. You immediately reach toward your ear and feel the loose flesh and the blood. Shock and disbelief immediately set in. Then, all of sudden, the man you came to arrest calmly touches your ear and heals it.

So the director's decision to have the guard stay seated and look puzzled about what just happened is quite powerful and dramatically "right." You can see in the guard's eyes the wonder with which he beholds this Jesus. It is not unlikely that this Temple guard, like others later in the story, experiences some sort of conversion after being healed by Christ.

31) After Peter cuts off the guard's ear, Jesus commands him to put away his sword with the famous words, "He who lives by the sword, dies by the sword." Did Jesus really say this?

Yes, He did. These famous words are found in Matthew 26:52. Aside from their surface meaning that one is likely to be killed by violence if one habitually commits violent acts, there is the deeper warning that one risks one's immortal soul by breaking the commandment, "You shall not kill."

32) Who is the group of Jewish leaders that pay Judas to betray Jesus?

The group is the Sanhedrin, the council of Jewish leaders made up of the priests, scribes, and elders. These groups did not always agree; each had its own agenda. But they were generally in agreement that Jesus was dangerous and needed to be silenced because He threatened their power with the people and with the Romans. The leader of the council was the high priest. The high priest at that time was named Caiaphas, and he played a pivotal role in convincing the council to condemn Jesus.

33) What was the Sanhedrin's motivation to do away with Jesus?

They had several motives. First, the Bible reveals that there was some jealousy on the part of the religious leaders. Jesus was an itinerant preacher; He was not a priest, scribe, or elder. In addition, the reports that Jesus performed incredible miracles, such as curing the blind and raising people from the dead, and spoke against the hypocrisy of the scribes and Pharisees undoubtedly frightened them. There were also instances when Jesus' actions seemed to contradict what they understood the Law to teach, such as His healing of a man on the Sabbath. In short, His popularity threatened their role as the leaders of the Jewish people.

Most importantly, though, Jesus spelled out in very clear terms that He was God's Son—an unthinkable blasphemy to the Sanhedrin. He claimed, for instance, to forgive sins. Not just sins against Himself, but any sins. He took the name of God ("I AM") for Himself, saying, "Before Abraham was, I AM" (John 8:58). He said He was coming at the end of time to judge the world. He accepted Messianic titles such as "Son of David," "Son of Man," and "Christ, Son of the Living God." These words and deeds certainly led to heated debates between Jesus and the Jewish religious leaders. And this inevitably led to a meeting of the Sanhedrin at which it was determined that Jesus' actions were stirring up the people and, as a result, would cause the Romans to replace them and further repress the Jewish nation. Caiaphas spoke their resolution: "It is expedient ... that one man should die for the people, and that the whole nation should not perish" (John 11:50).

His judgment seems almost reasonable in light of the harsh oppression of Roman rule, except, of course, for the part about condemning an innocent man—a man who repeatedly proved He was God's Son through the miracles He worked.

34) This film has stirred up controversy in some circles as to its portrayal of Jewish leaders. Do Catholics believe that the Jewish people bear collective guilt for Jesus' death?

Absolutely not. The official teaching of the Catholic Church concerning the question "Who is responsible for the death of Jesus?" is clear and unequivocal. Some misguided Christians (including, sadly, some Catholics) hold the notion that "the Jews are collectively responsible for the death of Jesus" and that they alone are to blame. This notion was clearly repudiated by the Second Vatican Council: "Neither all Jews indiscriminately at that time, nor Jews today, can be charged with the crimes committed during [Jesus'] Passion... the Jews should not be spoken of as rejected or accursed as if this followed from holy Scripture" (*Catechism of the Catholic Church*, paragraph 597).

To understand who is *really* responsible for Jesus' death, the Church says the best place for each of us to look is in the mirror. The *Catechism* tells us (paragraph 598): "... the Church has never forgotten that 'sinners were the authors and the ministers of all the sufferings that the divine Redeemer endured.' Taking into account the fact that our sins affect Christ Himself, the Church does not hesitate to impute to Christians the gravest responsibility for the torments inflicted upon Jesus, a responsibility with which they have all too often burdened the Jews alone:

> We must regard as guilty all those who continue to relapse into their sins. Since our sins made the Lord Christ suffer the torment of the cross, those who plunge themselves into disorders and crimes crucify the Son of God anew in their hearts (for He is in them) and hold Him up to contempt. And it can be seen that our crime in this case is greater in us than in the Jews. As for them, according to the witness of the Apostle, 'None of the rulers of this age understood this; for if they had, they would not have crucified the Lord of glory.' We, however, profess to know Him. And when we deny Him by our deeds, we in some way seem to lay violent hands on Him." (CCC 598)

This teaching is not, by the way, anything new or an invention of the Church in the 1960s. The proof? The quote above, which also appears in the *Catechism*, is from the documents of the Council of Trent in the mid-1500s. The following quote comes from St. Francis of Assisi in the 13th century—and was spoken to Christians, not Jews: "Nor did demons crucify Him; it is you who have crucified Him and crucify Him still, when you delight in your vices and sins."

In short, the responsibility for Christ's death lies with all the sinful children of Adam and Eve. The irony is that, in blaming Jews alone for the death of Jesus, Christian anti-Semites are, in effect, saying, "Jesus did not die because of my sins. He died because of Those People Over There." That is an absurd thing for a Christian to say. The truth, as the Catholic faith has always taught, is that "All sinners were the authors of Christ's Passion."

35) The director uses "flashbacks" to connect the Passion to other aspects of Jesus' life. The first flashback shows Jesus as a carpenter, living at home with His mother. What was the director's purpose in creating this scene?

Besides providing some relief from the mounting intensity, it appears that Mary's humanity and Jesus' divinity are each illustrated in Mary's comment that tall tables (such as those we use every day in our homes) will never catch on!

This poignant scene of loving interaction between Jesus and Mary helps us reflect on the marvelous fact that Jesus probably lived with His mother for His first thirty years. Despite being a divine Person, He was very "human" in how He lived. He ate. He worked as a carpenter. He had neighbors, family, and friends with whom He interacted like everybody else. He laughed and no doubt joked with His mother, as illustrated by the scene in which they splash water at each other. Seeing Mary's very normal motherly interaction with Jesus also brings home the depth of pain she must have experienced in witnessing His Passion.

36) When the film returns to the present—that is, when the persecution of Jesus by the Romans begins—we see Mary resolutely saying, "It has begun, Lord. So be it." Did Mary really know what was about to happen to her Son?

As a faithful Jewish woman, and as the virgin to whom the angel Gabriel appeared, Mary would have been well versed in the prophecies about the Messiah. Though neither Jesus' disciples nor the average Jew expected the Messiah to have to suffer to reign in glory, Mary's knowledge of Jesus' sufferings would more likely have come through her reflection on the unique prophecy she and Joseph received when they first presented Jesus at the Temple. The prophet Simeon told her that "a sword will pierce your heart" (Luke 2:35). This is clearly a prediction of the sorrow she would experience because of her Son's redemptive work.

37) Why is Jesus' father, Joseph, not shown in the film?

Perhaps if the director chose to include another flashback to Jesus' boyhood we would get a glimpse of Joseph. But the fact is that we hear no more about Joseph in the Bible after the twelve-year-old Jesus was found in the Temple. Most scholars believe that Joseph had died by the time Jesus began His mission, which seems likely in light of Jesus' placing His mother in the care of the apostle John.

38) Why is Pilate's wife, Claudia, portrayed as being so concerned about Jesus' fate?

There are probably two reasons: First, there is serious speculation that she was a "secret" Christian. Pilate, of course, would have known this, but probably few others would have. Secondly, she shows compassion (or at least wisdom) on the question of whether Christ should be crucified. In the Bible she warns her husband, "Have nothing to do with that righteous man, for I have suffered much over him today in a dream" (Matthew 27:19).

39) When Jesus is brought before Caiaphas and the council of elders, the final charge against him is "blasphemy." What is blasphemy?

According the *Catechism of the Catholic Church*, blasphemy is "directly opposed to the second commandment. It consists in uttering against God—inwardly or outwardly—words of hatred, reproach, or defiance; in speaking ill of God; in failing in respect toward [Him] in one's speech; in misusing God's name" (CCC 2148). The commandment against blasphemy also forbids us from speaking against the Church, the saints, and sacred things. Blasphemy is a grave sin.

40) Was the penalty for blasphemy really death? This seems awfully harsh.

The penalty for blaspheming God's name is written in the book of Leviticus: death by stoning (Leviticus 24:16). This law was written in the time of Moses when some Israelites were worshipping a golden calf instead of recognizing the true God who had miraculously led them out of slavery in Egypt.

Because of the Roman occupation, the Jewish authorities were not allowed to carry out the death penalty. This is why Jesus was taken to the Roman governor, Pontius Pilate. (It is interesting to note that Caiaphas persisted in getting a *crucifixion* order approved, rather than a stoning order. This suggests that he wasn't so much interested in seeing Jesus condemned according to the Law as he was about getting rid of Him by any means.)

41) One of the men testifying against Jesus argues that Jesus claimed He was "the Bread of Life," and repeatedly spoke about eating His flesh and drinking His blood. Where is this in the Bible?

This reference is to Jesus' lengthy discourse in the Gospel of John, chapter 6, where Jesus refers to Himself as "the Bread of Life" (John 6:48) and says that "unless you eat the flesh of the Son of Man and drink His blood, you have no life in you" (John 6:53). In response to this statement, many of Jesus' disciples stopped following Him. What is interesting is that Jesus allowed these disciples to leave Him. He did not call them back, saying "Hey, wait a minute. I didn't mean that *literally*. I meant it symbolically." He let them go because He really meant what He said.

The Catholic, Orthodox, and some Protestant churches accept that Jesus meant this teaching to be understood literally—namely, that He would give His very self to His followers as spiritual food. This food, however, would come to us in the humble form of bread and wine. Jesus professed this same teaching on the night before He was betrayed, Holy Thursday, when at the Last Supper He held up the bread, blessed and broke it, and gave it to His disciples, saying, "'Take; this is My body.' And He took a cup, and when He had given thanks He gave it to them, and they all drank of it. And He said to them, 'This is My blood of the covenant, which is poured out for many'" (Mark 14:22-24).

At first hearing, this teaching sounds strange ("unless you eat my flesh"). When we understand the background, however, it makes more sense. You may recall that the Passover was celebrated because the angel of death sent by God during the time of the ten plagues "passed over" every Hebrew home that had lamb's blood sprinkled on the doorpost. What is not commonly known, however, is that the families who killed the lamb and then sprinkled the lamb's blood also were told to *eat* the lamb. In order to complete the Paschal sacrifice, they had to eat the lamb that was slain. Jesus is the perfect Lamb. In order to share fully in His sacrifice on the cross, Christians are called to feed on the Lamb of God who is the Bread of Life.

42) During the mock trial, two Jewish leaders appear to be defending Jesus. Who are they?

While not identified in the movie, they are probably Nicodemus and Joseph of Arimathea. Both men are mentioned in the gospels as friendly to

Jesus and as secret disciples, out of fear of their fellow members of the Sanhedrin. Nicodemus actually came to Jesus at night to ask Him questions (John 3). We see the other man, Joseph of Arimathea, as Jesus is being taken down from the cross. Joseph, a wealthy follower of Jesus, gave up his tomb for Jesus' burial.

43) Was Jesus indeed guilty of blasphemy?

Jesus answered the chief priests' and scribes' questions by asking them to judge Him on the record of His public teaching. But when the high priest confronts Him point blank with the question, "Are you the Christ, the Son of the Blessed?" He states definitively that He is indeed the Son of Man and, more shocking, deliberately applies the Name of God to Himself ("I AM; and you will see the Son of Man seated at the right hand of Power, and coming with the clouds of heaven" [Mark 14: 62]). The high priest seizes on these words, tears his clothes, and declares that He has blasphemed. However, blasphemy would only apply if Jesus were lying! In fact, God Incarnate was standing right in front of them—just as Truth itself was standing before Pilate—and they did not recognize Him.

44) People today often take God's name in vain. Is this blasphemy?

Not exactly; at least not in most instances. But even though taking God's name in vain is not, strictly speaking, *blasphemy,* the second commandment forbids us from using God's name without the greatest reverence (see the *Catechism,* 2146). Though our jaded culture thinks nothing of it these days, we can be certain that God was serious when He gave us this commandment.

45) According to the Bible, Peter's denials took place while he was warming himself by the fire, which sounds like a rather quiet scene. Why is the scene portrayed so differently in this movie?

This is an example of the director's creative license being exercised to fully flesh out the emotion of the unfolding drama of Peter, leader of the disciples and future head of the Church.

46) Why does the director choose to have Peter fall at Mary's feet and cry out, "I have denied Him, Mother!"?

The intent here is probably to portray Catholic teaching that it is acceptable to appeal to Jesus' mother when you have offended God. Throughout the time of the Kings of Israel and Judah, the Queen Mother held a position of power and influence. To appeal to the mother of our King is eminently reasonable, since her heart and His are so closely bound together.

47) There is a scene in which Mary enters a place and finds Jesus chained to the ceiling below the stone pavement. What is the deeper significance of this scene?

One can imagine that the director seeks to portray in this image the eternal connection between Jesus and His mother. Jesus, the Messiah and fulfillment of ancient prophecy, and Mary, who abandoned herself to God's will from Jesus' birth to death, are permanently connected.

48) Is it a stretch to assume that Mary was an active participant in Christ's Passion?

Not at all. According to the Bible, Mary was present at some of Jesus' miracles, and in fact helped launch Jesus' public ministry by requesting that He provide wine for the presumably embarrassed hosts at the Cana wedding (John 2). Tradition has her meeting Jesus on His walk to Golgotha (where He was crucified) and Scripture also has her standing with Mary Magdalene and St. John at the foot of the cross.

49) Why do demon children surround Judas in his torment?

This is another creative device of the director. To portray something as innocent as young children at play in such a twisted and terrifying manner underscores the consequences of sin twisting our perception of the good, the true, and the beautiful. This has some important significance today since modern society, with its entrenched selfishness, has come to the view that children are a burden rather than a treasure, a curse rather than a blessing.

50) I presume the soldiers were Roman soldiers. If so, what was their relationship to the Jewish leaders?

Here's a political overview: The Romans had conquered this part of the world about a hundred years previously. It wasn't an important part of the Roman Empire by any means, as we see by Pontius Pilate's complaint in the movie about having been stationed there eleven long years! An unfriendly relationship existed between the Roman governor of the land of Judea, Pilate, and the Jewish leaders. The ace the Temple elite held up their sleeve was the threat of rioting. Pilate was under pressure from Caesar in Rome to keep the peace. Since the Jewish people expected the Messiah, foretold in their Scriptures, to be a *military* leader who would free them from occupation by their enemies (at this point in history, the Romans), this threat carried a lot of weight with Pilate. As a side note, the Jews were permitted a measure of police presence such as the temple guard, who arrested Jesus in the Garden.

51) Were the Roman soldiers really as brutal as they're portrayed in the film, or is this just a creation of Hollywood?

Records show that they were, indeed, that brutal. Crucifixion was perhaps the most painful and horrific means of execution ever devised. It was regularly practiced throughout the Roman Empire as a means of subduing the conquered populations. Jesus' case is a clear example of a situation that could be construed as having potential for an uprising. So a Jewish leader falsely accused Jesus of inciting a tax protest against Caesar in order to provoke the Roman sentence of crucifixion.

52) Pilate sends Jesus to another man in hopes that he would judge Jesus' innocence or guilt. Who is this man?

This smooth yet sinister character is Herod Antipas, the Jewish king who earlier had John the Baptist arrested because John condemned Herod's marriage to his own brother's wife. One day, the king's step-daughter, Salome, so pleased him with a seductive dance that he asked her what he could give her as a reward.   At her mother's prompting, she asked for the head of John the Baptist. Herod reluctantly complied and had John executed (Matthew 14: 3-12). During the time of Jesus, Herod ruled the Jewish population in the region of Galilee under an agreement with the Romans.

53) Why did Pilate send Jesus to King Herod? Why didn't he judge him himself?

Probably because he knew that Jesus was innocent and that the Jewish authorities had handed Him over due to jealousy. As a result, he was disinclined to pass judgment on Jesus. Also, Pilate's wife, Claudia, told him to have nothing to do with that righteous man (see Matthew 27:19). A jurisdictional technicality initially got him off the hook: Jesus was from the land of Galilee, and as such was under the primary authority of King Herod. In the end, however, Pilate was forced to pass judgment after Herod refused to take any action.

54) Should Christians condemn Pilate for his actions? He seemed to have done the best he could under the circumstances.

Although political decisions can be difficult, those blessed with authority are called to follow the narrow path, act justly, and defend what is good and true regardless of the consequences. Pilate acted out of fear and self-interest—he had been installed as governor to keep the peace in Jerusalem, and it looked as if the crowd would riot and, more importantly to him, he would get in trouble with Caesar and lose his hard-won career, unless he handed over Jesus to be crucified. Though he tried repeatedly to release Jesus, Pilate in the end sought His own good rather than the ultimate good. He "washed his hands" of Jesus' condemnation and death, but he still bears great responsibility for it. He could have declared Jesus innocent and released Him; instead, he permitted the murder of the Author of life itself.

55) Why does Jesus remain silent before Herod?

This strange event has often been explained in this way: Herod was so dedicated to depravity and sin that any attempt by Jesus to reach him would have been fruitless. Jesus certainly knew of Herod's taking his brother's wife as his own and of his role in the murder of John the Baptist. In essence, since Herod would not play any direct role in the saving events that would follow, Jesus had merely to suffer the fool without engaging him directly. There is also a profound theological point to be made here regarding Jesus' silence—as the *Catechism* notes, Jesus is "the suffering Servant [of Isaiah 53:7] who silently allows himself to be led to the slaughter..." (CCC 608).

56) The movie includes a scene in which Pilate asks his wife about "truth" and why he can't hear it. Why?

This tender scene beautifully portrays the reality that truth is written on men's hearts. The prophet Jeremiah and the apostle Paul in the Bible discuss this idea most eloquently. The scene also emphasizes that Pilate may have been sincere in his question to Jesus: "What is truth?" It gives the impression that

Pilate was profoundly disturbed—even haunted—by Jesus and truly distressed about the role he found himself playing in this drama. Nevertheless, whatever distress he felt, he still used his authority to have the innocent God-Man crucified.

57) After Pilate proclaims that neither he nor Herod has found fault with Jesus, we are introduced to the criminal Barabbas. Why does Pilate offer to release a prisoner at that point?

He does this simply because it was his custom to release a prisoner every year at Passover as a gesture of Roman "good will." This was the optimal time from a public relations standpoint to make such a gesture because Jerusalem was filled with pilgrims from many lands who had come to celebrate the Passover.

The release of Barabbas is troubling because he was a known murderer and political zealot—a clear danger to the Roman state. His release added insult to injury. Jesus' own people, for whom He had demonstrated great love and worked many miracles, chose to free a murderer rather than the innocent Son of God. (It is interesting to note that the name *Barabbas* literally means "son of the father." This is particularly ironic in that the true "Son of the Father"—Jesus—was standing right in front of them.)

58) The most powerful (and, frankly, the most difficult) part of the movie to watch is the whipping of Jesus. Why did the director make this scene so violent?

Historical records indicate that the practice of scourging was horrible and very bloody. In our own land, the experience of African American slaves during several hundred years of bondage bears witness to this fact. Also, the evidence from the Shroud of Turin—believed by many to be the actual burial cloth of Jesus—shows that the back of the man on the shroud was severely bruised and bloodied. The director's stated intention in making *The Passion of The Christ* was to show the brutal reality of what Jesus actually experienced.

One simply needs to see the instruments of scourging to understand something of its horror. In Pierre Barbet's book, *A Doctor at Calvary*, we find this description:

> ...a distinctively Roman instrument was used; the flagrum. It had a short handle, to which were attached several long, thick thongs, usually two of them. At a little distance from the end balls of lead or the small bones of sheep were inserted...The thongs would cut the skin and the balls and the little bones would dig deep contused wounds into it. There would be a good deal of hemorrhage and considerable lowering of vital resistance.

In the movie, the devil is present at Jesus' scourging. We see Satan holding a grotesque baby demon in his arms and swirling around the action of this sequence, inciting the torturers to maximum violence and brutality. This was the devil's moment, in which he thought he was winning the battle with God.

59) Why is the scene so long?

Because the scourging took about that long. It was so brutal that it nearly succeeded in killing Jesus prior to His crucifixion. The scourging of Jesus is not something we should turn away from or avoid; it is a powerful reality we should meditate on. One fruitful way of doing so is by praying the Rosary, which is a meditation on the life of Christ. This fruitful prayer is divided into twenty "mysteries." The *sorrowful mysteries* focus on key events in the Passion of Jesus: His agony in the garden, scourging, crowning with thorns, carrying of the cross, crucifixion and death. Praying these mysteries will open your heart to experiencing the profound meaning of Christ's Passion and help you apply it to your life.

60) What is the significance of the flashback in which Jesus washes His disciples' feet?

Jesus came to serve and to teach us how to live. The lesson He imparts in this scene is that, although He is God, He humbled Himself for our benefit; He, the Lord of the Universe, became a servant to His creation. By this action of washing His disciples' feet, Jesus shows us the nature of true love: dying to ourselves and living for others. If we do this, we discover who we truly are. The way of love is sacrifice—the laying down of one's life for others in ways big and small, including the humble act of washing another's feet.

61) Why does the movie show Pilate's wife giving Mary an armful of towels?

This is a beautiful artistic device which visually portrays a devotion to the precious blood of Christ— the blood that was shed for us, the blood that saves us. The Bible says, "by [Jesus'] wounds we are healed" (1 Peter 2:24).

Mary, as a mother, demonstrates here more than just a maternal love of her Son; she shows her understanding of the sacredness of His blood.

62) In the scene in which Jesus saves the woman caught in adultery from being stoned, we see Him writing in the sand. What is the significance of this act?

This scene is taken directly from the New Testament (John 8:3-11). Some theologians and biblical scholars have speculated that Jesus was perhaps writing down the sins of the men who were about to stone her. Others note that Jesus' action recalls the One who gave the Law in the first place on Mount Sinai, for Exodus describes the Ten Commandments (including "You shall not commit adultery") being written in stone by the "finger of God." Therefore it is fitting that the One who gave the Law, now grants mercy. At any rate, it is from this incident we get the challenging words, "Let him who is without sin ... be the first to throw a stone at her" (John 8:7).

63) Before we leave the scourging scene, please explain the meaning of the baby demon that is being held by the devil.

This is yet another example of artistic license taken by the director. Its symbolism is both disconcerting and powerful. Here are a few likely interpretations: first, the devil wants to corrupt anything that is good and beautiful in God's creation. The image of the hideous demon child could simply be seen as a very tangible depiction of moral ugliness. A second interpretation would be to show the gift of life—a human child—in such a depraved manner. This image could very well be symbolic of our contemporary culture's frequent disdain of children (as revealed through the widespread acceptance of abortion and the reality of child abuse). A final interpretation of this scene is the contrast between Mary's gazing on her child, Jesus, and Satan's embracing of this child. You probably also noticed the smile on the demon child's face. This sends the message to the audience that he is delighting in Jesus' suffering.

64) Did Pilate think that, by exclaiming, *"Ecce homo!"*—"Behold the man!"—and showing Jesus' torment, the crowd's bloodlust would be satisfied?

Here we see a vivid contrast between a man who still has a shred of compassion left in his heart set against a seething mob whose appetites for greater spectacle can't be satiated. Sadly, this is a perceptive portrayal of the human condition: our appetites for sin and vice, once we indulge them, grow ever stronger and can never, ultimately, be satisfied.

65) Why is a contrast established between Pilate's "washing his hands" and Jesus purifying His hands at the Last Supper?

To "wash one's hands" of responsibility for something is a popular expression in our culture that comes directly from this historic event. Pilate "washes his hands" of Jesus' imminent crucifixion to show that, in his mind, he bears no responsibility for it (see Matthew 27:24). In this symbolic act, Pilate says that he has tried to do what is right and have Jesus released, but that the Temple authorities and the crowd would not allow him. So now he's done with the matter; whatever happens is not his fault. The contrast here points to the crucial difference between performing a God-given duty (God required in the Old Testament that people purify their hands before eating) and avoiding one's God-given responsibility (judging justly).

66) Why does one of the condemned men with Jesus make fun of Jesus when He first embraces His cross on the road to Calvary?

This scene is not revealed in the Bible. It is another example of the director's creative license. As Jesus and the two men condemned with Him are given their crosses and begin the difficult journey to Calvary, one of the two men mocks Jesus as He picks up His cross. This man—known in tradition as "the bad thief"—obviously does not understand that suffering must be embraced if we are to grow in our love and trust of God. In the Father's providence, all things work for the good of those who love Him (see Romans 8:28). While we can accept suffering that results from our own poor choices, it is the suffering that comes our way through no fault of our own that can most severely try our faith. God's ways are beyond our understanding. But our Christian faith teaches us the necessity of embracing the cross, of accepting all that God permits to happen so that we might be purged of self-will and conform to His will more fully. This is the path to holiness and salvation.

67) At one point along the way of the cross, Jesus seems almost to caress His cross. Did I see that right?

Again, as absolutely confounding as this is to our modern sensibilities, the Catholic Church recognizes the redemptive value of suffering. Jesus teaches that suffering is inescapable and transforming, and we need to welcome and embrace it. It has redemptive value when we offer it to God, meaning that we participate with God in the atonement of our sins (see Colossians 1:24).

68) As Jesus carries His cross, the director cross-cuts between the devil and Mary walking along with Him on opposite sides through the crowd. At one point, their eyes meet in an amazingly powerful silent exchange. What exactly is going on here?

Catholics recognize Mary's obedience to God as the antithesis of the devil's rebellion against God. This is a shock to many people, who think that the *devil* is the opposite of God. But nothing is the opposite of God, for God has no equals. Nor, apart from God, could Mary be the devil's opponent since the devil, as an angel, is vastly more powerful than any human being, naturally speaking. But Mary is "full of grace" as Gabriel called her. She is full of the life of God and is therefore able to confront the devil, not only during the Passion, but for our sake as well, now that she is glorified in heaven. The angel Gabriel appeared to her when she was a teenager, announcing God's will that she become the mother of the Messiah. Her "yes" to God brought the world the gift of salvation—the Incarnate Son of God, Jesus. Her immediate "yes" to God stands in direct opposition to Lucifer's rejection of God's will.

Mary's "yes" also stands in stark contrast to Eve's "no" to God in the Garden of Eden. While in the book of Genesis Eve is seduced by the devil, Mary thwarts the devil's plans by accepting God's will for her beloved Son. This is why Christians traditionally refer to Mary as the "new Eve"— her "yes" (obedience) to God cancelled out Eve's "no" (sin and rebellion) and began humanity's restoration to grace.

This scene of Jesus' walk to Calvary illustrates the battle that was (and still is) taking place between Mary and the devil. The devil despises Mary because of her role in giving the world its Savior, her purity of heart, her role as intercessor before God, and her total faithfulness. Evidence of this hatred towards "the woman" is revealed at both the beginning and end of the Bible. In Genesis, we hear God reveal that He will "put enmity between you [the devil, represented by the serpent] and the woman" (Genesis 3:15). In the book of Revelation, we see that the devil (represented by the dragon) desires to devour the woman's child, but she flees into the desert (see Revelation 12:6). The "woman" spoken of here is an allusion, not only to Mary, God's specially chosen woman, but to Israel, the "Virgin Daughter of Zion" of whom Mary is the supreme example, and to the Church, of whom Mary is the supreme icon and image.

69) Do Catholics worship Mary?

No. Catholics *honor* Mary and recognize her as the greatest of all the saints. She is, quite simply, the new "Ark of the Covenant," the vessel whom God chose to carry His Son, and is therefore worthy of great respect and devotion. Just as the Ark of the Covenant in the Old Testament held the word of God (the tablets of the Ten Commandments) and the bread from heaven (the *manna*), so too did Mary hold in her womb the Word of God and the Bread of Heaven—Jesus.

Because of her special closeness to God, Catholics ask for her special intercession with God on our behalf. This is in large part why devotion to Mary is so important to our spiritual lives.

70) I've heard of the Stations of the Cross, and I believe they commemorate some of the events seen in the film. What exactly are the Stations?

A traditional and popular Catholic devotion, the Stations of the Cross have been prayerfully practiced in one form or another for nearly 1,000 years.

The Stations recall fourteen key events or points along Jesus' walk to Calvary, the place of His crucifixion. They allow us to "walk along" spiritually with Jesus during His final hours. Among the events commemorated are Jesus' condemnation by Pilate, His taking up of the cross and falling three times, and His meeting with His mother. The actual prayers prayed at each station vary; there are many "versions" of these prayers. Some are reflections composed by saints from centuries ago; others are more contemporary in their wording.

Images of the Stations of the Cross can be found in nearly all Catholic churches in the world. They appear in various artistic styles, both ancient and modern.

71) How far was Jesus' walk to Calvary?

Jesus' path to Calvary is known as the *Via Dolorosa* or "Way of Sorrows." This road from the Praetorium (the Roman judgment hall) to Calvary, the hill that was the site of the crucifixion, is about 650 yards long—a little more than 1/3 of a mile. Its surface would have been very rough and the carrying of a heavy beam—after the scourging at the pillar— would have been exceedingly difficult for Jesus.

Over the centuries, millions of people have walked this path in devotion to the Passion. If you go to Jerusalem, daily pilgrimages are made from the Monastery of the Flagellation to Calvary.

72) During Jesus' carrying of the cross, a woman breaks through the crowd to help Jesus and wipes His face. Who is this woman?

Her name is Veronica. This event, though not revealed in the Bible, is a common story which has been retold and celebrated by the faithful.

73) Is the scene where Jesus' bloody face is imprinted on Veronica's veil an artistic device of the filmmaker?

No. According to the historical record, the veil of Veronica has been seen and venerated over the centuries. Some speculate that this image is the primary source for understanding what Jesus actually looked like. In Christian tradition, Veronica kept the veil and discovered its curative properties. It is said that she cured the Roman emperor Tiberius from illness with the veil, then left it in the care of Pope Clement (the third successor of St. Peter) and his successors.

74) Has Veronica's veil survived to this day?

Some question exists as to whether Veronica's veil is actually in St. Peter's Basilica as is traditionally thought. There, beside the main altar, one will find a statue of Veronica with a Latin inscription saying the veil is preserved within.

A brief history: As early as the fourth century, Church documents reflected the existence of the veil, and in the Holy Year of 1300, the veil of Veronica was publicly displayed in Rome. The veil was typically described as being made of thin material with an image on both sides of a person with eyes wide open and a face full of suffering and with noticeable blood spots. The historical difficulty begins in 1608 when the chapel where the veil was kept was demolished by Pope Paul V in the rebuilding of St. Peter's Basilica. At that point, some speculate the veil was stolen. In 1616, Pope Paul V prohibited copies of Veronica's veil not made by a canon (priest) of St. Peter's Basilica. In fact, all the copies made after this period bore the image of Christ with His eyes closed, though earlier images show Christ with His eyes open. So the short answer is that scholars remain uncertain as to whether the actual veil has survived.

75) **I couldn't help but notice that all four principal female characters in the movie are presented in a very positive light. Is this a bow to political correctness on the part of the filmmaker?**

The film's positive depiction of women was intentional on the part of the director. But far from caving to any demands of political correctness, the director is instead reflecting a mixture of both Catholic teaching and common Catholic piety about these women. Scripture tells us that the Blessed Virgin Mary and Mary Magdalene were present at the Passion of Christ. Catholic pious tradition also includes the figures of Veronica and Claudia, the wife of Pilate. What both Scripture and Tradition agree on is that nearly all the men in Christ's life (with the exception of the apostle John) ran away. This is a fact worthy of deeper consideration and meditation.

76) Who is the man who helps Jesus carry His cross? Is he mentioned in the Bible?

We know from the Bible that he was Simon of Cyrene, a town located on the North African coast. It is likely that he was a pilgrim in Jerusalem for the Passover festival, as Jews from many lands would converge on Jerusalem for important feast days. Simon's mention in Scripture is brief. We are told simply that he was the one "forced" by the Roman soldiers to help Jesus carry the cross (see Luke 23: 26), though the Gospel of Mark also tells us the names of his sons, Alexander and Rufus (see Mark 15:21). Catholic tradition, however, goes on to tell us that this man, chosen in God's plan to play such an intimate role in alleviating Jesus' burden, experienced a powerful conversion to Christianity.

In a sense, Simon of Cyrene represents all of us—we are all called by Jesus to pick up our cross daily and follow Him (see Luke 9:23). Jesus invites each of us to participate in His redeeming work through the sacrificial offering of our lives.

77) At what point in His public ministry did Jesus say, "If you only love those who love you, what reward is in that?"

The Sermon on the Mount (found in Matthew, chapters 5-7) proclaims the arrival of God's

Kingdom and summarizes the heart of Jesus' teachings. The quote in question is from Matthew 5: 46, in which Jesus discusses the true nature of love.

78) I heard a historian say that Jesus only carried the crossbeam—the horizontal part of the cross—as He walked to Calvary. Why does the movie show Him carrying the whole cross?

In Roman practice, it was customary to have those condemned to crucifixion carry only the crossbeam—*the patibulum*—to the place of execution. Once there, the horizontal patibulum would be attached to the vertical post and the entire cross would be raised. So it is almost certain that Jesus would have done the same.

Because, however, so much of Christian art over the past 1,000 years portrays Jesus carrying the whole cross, the director chose to show Him carrying the cross in this manner. The crossbeam, which would normally weigh between 50 and 100 pounds, would have been torture enough. The director's choice doesn't seem to be an attempt to make things look worse, but simply to make use of an image already in the viewer's mind to connect to the historical event.

79) Wouldn't the nails have been driven into Jesus' wrists—not His hands—so as to support the weight of His body? The movie shows the nails going into His hands.

During a typical Roman crucifixion, it is generally understood the nails were placed into the wrists and not the hands. The decision of the director to show the nails going into Christ's hands is yet another example of artistic license, probably chosen for the same reason Jesus is depicted as carrying the "whole" cross: the influence of Christian art, which has traditionally shown Jesus with the nails in His hands. The two possibilities are equally dreadful, so the director's choice is of little consequence. (It is interesting to note that the Shroud of Turin is historically accurate on this point: the man whose body appears on the Shroud has wounds in his wrist, not his hands.)

80) Does the director, Mel Gibson, appear in the film?

Yes. Gibson's left hand is seen holding the nail that is driven into one of Jesus' hands. He has explained that he did this to dramatize the point that it was his own sinfulness, at least in part, that crucified Christ.

81) What else do we know about the Roman practice of crucifixion?

After arrival at the place of execution, the typical Roman crucifixion began with the removal of the person's clothes and the fixing of the wrists to the crossbeam with long nails. The condemned man's feet would then be nailed to a piece of wood attached to the vertical beam. Though all of this was excruciatingly painful, none of these wounds would be fatal. Death would occur from the weight of the victim's body eventually causing exhaustion and asphyxiation. The victim would literally suffocate. The Romans themselves so clearly recognized the exceptional cruelty of crucifixion as a method of execution that Roman citizens convicted of capital crimes and sentenced to death were always beheaded, never crucified.

82) Why the awful, disgusting bird shots in the crucifixion scene?

In order to provide another historical detail. Carnivorous birds and birds of prey would often descend on the victims of crucifixion. It is also believed that some victims died from attacks by dogs. The fate of the "bad thief" is also meant to contrast with that of the "good thief," who in the Bible professes belief in Christ at the eleventh hour and is assured by Jesus of a share in His Kingdom.

83) Why does the movie show a flashback to the Last Supper during the crucifixion?

The way Jesus celebrated the Passover meal (i.e., the Last Supper) with His apostles was meant to fulfill the Old Covenant. He declared that the Passover bread was His body and the wine His blood. He required that this new ritual be practiced in memory of Him. We know this today as the Eucharist or Holy Communion. Jesus speaks at length in Chapter 6 of John's Gospel about how His flesh is real food and blood real drink, perplexing many of His followers at the time. The once-and-for-all sacrifice of His body on the cross is "re-presented" tangibly on earth by the sacrifice on the altar, the bread and wine that become His Body and Blood. This ritual is referred to as "the breaking of the bread" in the New Testament (Acts 2:42) and in the writings of the early Church Fathers.

A new meaning is given to the Passover because its purpose has been fulfilled. The Son of God—the spotless, sinless Lamb—has become the sacrifice.

Consuming the Passover meal in its new form—the Eucharist—is made the requirement to have life within you. "I am the Bread of Life; he who comes to me shall not hunger" (John 6:35). See John 6:22-71 for Jesus' full explanation of this core teaching.

84) Please explain the strange scene in which the cross on which Jesus has just been nailed is flipped over but remains suspended above the ground.

The Venerable Maria de Agreda (1602-1665), a Spanish nun, included this startling detail in her mystical writings about the life of Mary, the mother of Jesus. The film borrows picturesque details from her works and also from the meditations of Ven. Anne Catherine Emmerich (1774-1824) on Christ's Passion. The "visions" of these two nuns sometimes have a symbolic rather than a literal meaning. While the Catholic Church has never declared them to be supernatural revelations, it has allowed them to be published. For centuries they have inspired genuine devotion to the truths of the faith.

85) Did Jesus die more quickly than was normal for crucifixion?

It would seem so. The Bible states that Jesus was on the cross for three hours before He died (see Matthew 27:45-46)—a relatively short period of time, considering that many lingered for days before dying. But we need to remember that Jesus, as the God-Man, *chose* the moment of His death. He freely lays down His life for us; it is not taken from Him by men. It is when Jesus says "It is accomplished" that He gives up His spirit in death.

86) What words are written on the sign that is nailed above Jesus' head?

Placed on the cross by order of Pontius Pilate and written in Hebrew, Latin, and Greek, the sign reads: "Jesus of Nazareth, King of the Jews" (see John 19: 19-20). The letters usually seen on a crucifix are INRI – an abbreviation of the Latin *Iesus Nazarenus, Rex Iudaeorum*. Though not portrayed in the film, the Bible tells us that the Jewish leaders returned to Pilate and demanded that the sign be changed to read: *"This man said,* 'I am the King of the Jews'" (John 19:21). But Pilate dismissed them, saying, "What I have written, I have written" (John 19:22). The Church of the Holy Cross in Rome houses various relics of the Passion including what appears to be a piece of this sign.

87) What is the meaning of Jesus' dramatic words from the cross, *"Eloi, Eloi, lama sabachthani"*?

These are Aramaic words meaning "My God, my God, why have you forsaken me?" From the depths of His human nature, Jesus cries out in anguish to His Father. Some have misinterpreted these words to mean that Jesus was in despair, and had not expected the crucifixion. We must be careful here, though, not to draw an inaccurate conclusion about Jesus, namely, that He is not divine or is somehow less than God. This is not the proper understanding of His words of abandonment. Jesus, as a divine Person, knew the plan of salvation from all eternity; He shares the same nature as the Father and the Holy Spirit.

Rather, what we see here is the true humanity of Jesus. He didn't just look like us, but also felt everything we feel. The pain He experienced on the cross was not merely physical; it was profoundly spiritual as He took on the weight of all human sins, past, present, and future.

Though He may have experienced great emotional desolation as well as physical suffering on the cross, the words "My God, my God, why have you forsaken me?" are actually the first words of Psalm 22. Jesus here is pointing to the fact that what is happening to Him is a fulfillment of this prophetic psalm, which predicts the piercing of His hands and feet and the casting lots for His clothes. The psalm concludes with a triumphant, confident proclamation of eventual vindication by God.

88) Does the movie give us all that Jesus said from the cross?

No, not all of His words are included in *The Passion of The Christ*. For a full list of Jesus' seven last "words" (sayings), see Appendix C—The Seven Last Words of Christ.

89) Explain why the film flashes back to Jesus offering the wine at the Last Supper as His blood drips down to the foot of the cross.

As Jesus raised the wine at the Last Supper, He said, "All of you must drink from it, for this is my blood, the blood of the covenant, to be poured out on behalf of many for the forgiveness of sins" (Matthew 26: 28). This pouring out of Jesus' blood on the cross constitutes the sacrifice necessary to atone for all the sins of mankind. Because of Jesus' command to "Do this in memory of Me," the Eucharist takes place every day on every altar in every Catholic church around the world, as well as in the liturgy of the Orthodox Church.

90) Was Jesus really taunted by one of the crucified criminals beside Him, or is this provided in the film for dramatic effect?

The Bible records that one of the men said to Him, "Are you not the Christ? Save yourself and us!" (Luke 23:39). Catholic tradition calls the other crucified man—the "good thief"—Dismas. He responds to the first criminal's words by saying, "Do you not fear God, since you are under the same sentence of condemnation? And we indeed justly; for we are receiving the due reward of our deeds; but this man [Jesus] had done nothing wrong....Jesus, remember me when you come in your kingly power" (Luke 23:40-42). Jesus then responds with words to Dismas: "Truly, I say to you, today you will be with Me in paradise" (Luke 23:43). The forgiveness of Dismas by Jesus gives all Christians hope in the saving power of faith. Even at the hour of death it is possible to ask for and receive forgiveness of one's sins by trusting in Jesus!

91) If He was indeed God, why didn't Jesus perform another miracle by coming down off the cross? Surely that would have made believers out of His enemies!

Not necessarily. Lazarus had recently been raised by Jesus in a public spectacle after being dead in the tomb for four days (see John 11). A blind man had been healed right in the middle of Jerusalem (John 9). Christ's enemies responded by calling the blind man a liar and throwing him out of the synagogue.

Clearly, spectacular displays don't always inspire faith. Seeing is not always believing. But, more to the point, if Jesus *had* come down from the cross, He would have nullified the very reason for His coming into the world—to save us from our sins and make eternal life in heaven possible for us. He needed to remain on the cross until death in order to offer the sacrificial atonement required to reconcile us with God and break our bondage to sin.

92) What is the significance of Jesus' last words to His mother and the apostle John?

In saying "Woman, behold your son," and to John (the "beloved disciple" as the gospel calls him), "Behold your mother" (John 19:26-27), Jesus establishes His mother Mary as the spiritual mother of all Christians. We know from both the Bible and Tradition that John was not Mary's son by birth, so Jesus' words cannot be taken literally. John the Evangelist describes this incident because he wants us to see ourselves there in his place. Mary, mother of Jesus, is given to *us* as *our* mother.

For additional information on theological questions about Mary, see the Resources section.

93) Why does Jesus say, "It is accomplished," while He remains on the cross?

Love involves fidelity, which means faithfulness, even to the end. *The Catechism of the Catholic Church* teaches that Jesus' "love to the end" (see John 13:1) gives His sacrifice on the cross its redemptive value (CCC 616).

These words of Jesus are so rich that they afford a variety of meanings. The most obvious, though, is that Christ's Passion is now complete. He has completed the mission for which He came into the world to accomplish, namely to save humanity from its sins; to win back that which had been lost. The redemption of man has been accomplished. All men and women now have the opportunity to receive eternal life if they accept His grace and remain faithful until the end.

94) Why is there darkness, a thunderstorm, and an earthquake as Jesus dies?

To signify the magnitude of what has just occurred—the death of the God-Man. These are not merely dramatic additions to the film. Both darkness and the earthquake are described in the New Testament (see Matthew 27:45, 54). Moreover, in the Old Testament, the prophet Amos speaks of both the darkness and the earthquake. "Shall not the land tremble because of this...On that day, says the Lord God, I will make the sun set at midday and cover the earth with darkness in broad daylight" (Amos 8:8-9).

95) What happens in the Temple that so badly shocks the Jewish leaders?

The Temple veil rips in two from top to bottom revealing the sacred "Holy of Holies," in which God's presence dwelled and no man was permitted to enter except the High Priest once a year on *Yom Kippur* (the Day of Atonement). With the death of Christ, who is the True High Priest and the True Sacrifice, the separation between God and man ends, and we can now approach Him without fear and have communion with Him through grace.

96) Why does the devil react in such a frenzied manner to Christ's death on the Cross?

It appears that the devil, in the frightening isolation this scene depicts, is expressing rage and torment at his defeat. The devil's prediction in the Garden about the inability of one man to "bear the full burden of sin" was proved false—Jesus was actually able to go through with the Passion and to accomplish His redemptive mission. The devil was completely defeated at Calvary.

97) There seems to be a conversion of a Roman soldier at the end. What do we know of him?

Scripture records that one of the soldiers present at the crucifixion was so moved by the way Jesus died that he declared, "Surely this was a righteous man." Another gospel writer tells us he said, "Truly this man was the Son of God!" Catholic tradition tells us that this soldier became a Christian. The book and movie *The Robe* portray this soldier as the winner of the dice toss for Jesus' robe.

98) The heart-wrenching shot near the end of the film of Mary at the foot of the cross staring straight at us while holding her dead Son is very moving. What does it mean?

One could argue that this scene is the cinematic equivalent of Michelangelo's "Pieta" in its beauty and poignancy. It drives home the point through Mary's wounded, loving gaze that our collective sins killed her Son, but that His death has brought hope to mankind.

99) The movie closes with the Resurrection. Do Christians really believe that Jesus rose from the dead?

Yes, we do. The Resurrection is one of the most important dogmas of the Catholic faith. St. Paul states this most eloquently in his first letter to the Corinthians: "If Christ has not been raised [from the dead], then our preaching is in vain and your faith is in vain" (1 Corinthians 15:14). It is only in His resurrection that Jesus conquers the power of death and gives us the hope that our own bodies will be raised. Our hope of eternal life, then, rests upon our belief in the resurrection of Christ.

100) What happens after Jesus leaves the tomb?

Read the Gospels and the Acts of the Apostles to find out!

PART 2
THE CASE FOR CHRIST

We live in a pluralistic society, one in which a wide variety of religious expressions is the norm. In such a society, many believe that all paths lead to God; that one religion is as good as another. This would be true if all "paths" were merely man-made. And, if all religions *were* created by men, it would be arrogant to claim that one path is truer than another. But what if a particular path was not of merely human origin? What if one path *was* given to us directly by God?

Both history and God's Word—the Bible and Sacred Tradition—have revealed that one person among all others was unique. His name was Jesus Christ. The main difference between Jesus and, say, Buddha, or Muhammad, or Confucius, is that they never claimed to be or showed themselves to be divine. Through His preaching and miracles, Jesus showed that He was indeed the Messiah, the eternal Word of God who, at a specific time in human history, became flesh and dwelt among us.

The best known religious figures (such as Buddha, Muhammad, and Confucius) proclaimed the truth in many real—but partial—ways. Some of them, not all, even proclaimed the truth that there is one God. In short, it is one thing to *talk* about God. Many great and good people have done so over the ages. Jesus, though, is different; He *claimed to be God.*

That is a claim that has to be dealt with somehow. It cannot simply be ignored. That is why the central question in the Gospels is the question Jesus Himself put to His disciples: "Who do you say I am?" The case for Christ rests on the various claims people have made in response to that question. For there are really only **five possibilities**, and they all start with the letter "L."

Jesus was either:

1) a **legend**—that is, He never really existed; the New Testament is just a fable.

2) a **liar**—in effect, He didn't really mean the things He said. He was simply trying to pull a fast one on the people for personal gain.

3) a **lunatic**—that is, His claims to be God were merely the ranting of a crazy mind.

4) a **light and fluffy New Ager**—that is, He was trying to tell us we are all gods.

5) the **Lord**—He was who He claimed to be: the Son of God, God incarnate.

Now, let's examine each of these possibilities:

1) Jesus was just a **legend**.

> The problem with calling Jesus a "legend" is that no reputable historian in the world would say Jesus never existed. We know when the documents of the New Testament were written. As was discussed previously, most of the New Testament was written when the eyewitnesses to the events of Jesus' life, death and resurrection were still alive. And the telling thing about not only the authors, but also the people who preserved their writings over the centuries, is how little interest they seem to have had in "adjusting" history in order to create a legend.

Think about it: If the apostles were enthusiasts who just got a bit excited and mistook their rabbi for God, then why do the Gospel accounts show the disciples to be slow to understand His message and put their faith in Him?

Clearly we are looking at neither theological rocket scientists nor overly spiritual hysterics. In fact, the biblical documents continually paint a picture of the apostles as men who were a little slow on the uptake, as rather typically ambitious, and as cowards who abandoned the one they loved at the moment of His supreme crisis (Mark 14:50). It's highly unlikely that these men "puffed up" the story of Jesus for their own personal gain. Think about it: If you wanted to start your own new religious movement—touting the wonders of your leader—would you realistically show your leader in a negative light?

Followers who are trying to burnish the historical record and turn a mere human rabbi into a god would not be likely to carefully preserve Christ's last words: "My God, my God, why have you forsaken me?" (Matthew 27:46; Mark 15:34). Nor would they allow the editing scissors to miss quotes such as: "'Why do you call me good?' said Jesus, 'No one is good—except God alone'"(Mark 10:18); "He *could not* do many miracles there, except lay hands on a few sick people and heal them"(Mark 6:5); and "Who touched me?" (Luke 8:45). Such quotes appear, at first glance, to bear witness to Jesus' imperfection, weakness, and ignorance—not what you want when you are inventing a god.

So if the people who wrote (and preserved) the Gospels were not religious maniacs, cultists, liars, fact-fudgers, or historical revisionists, what were they? How about "honest men"? And these honest men tell us something astonishing: Jesus claimed to be God.

2) Jesus was a **liar**.

OK, so maybe the apostles told what they believed to be true. Isn't it still possible that *Jesus* was the deceiver here? Maybe He was just a clever huckster bent on selling Himself to the crowd for the usual reasons of power and money.

Problem is, Jesus does not do the things that a deceiver or opportunist would do. He flees into the desert when people try to make Him king (John 6: 15). Then He makes speeches (see John 6:25-60) that are guaranteed to offend all but the most die-hard grassroots supporters. He repeatedly conceals His miracles (Mark 5:43; 7:36; Luke 5:14). He hobnobs with thieves, drunkards, and lepers. He surrounds Himself with tacky people who would look terrible in campaign brochures. He looks past the president of the Capernaum Chamber of Commerce and, without excusing Himself, extends a cheery "Hello!" to a local prostitute who just crashed the exclusive cocktail party without an invitation (Luke 7:36-50). That's not the way to win political favor. Nor does it make sense to take particular pains to make sure that those Roman and Jewish leaders who thought the least of Him— and had the power to do something about it—would find plenty of reasons (and opportunities) to see Him dead.

Such political "blunders" characterized His entire career. He regularly alienated the most powerful men of His day, both Jewish and Roman:

> *Again the high priest asked him, "Are you the Christ, the Son of the Blessed One?" "I am,"* said Jesus (Mark 14:61-62).

> *And Pilate asked Him, "Are you the king of the Jews?"*
> *And [Jesus] answered him, "You have said so"* (Mark 15:2).

He was not a man to quibble about what the meaning of "is" is. Instead, when He was on trial for His life, He twice said the very thing that would absolutely ensure He suffered an ignominious and horrible death. If He was after worldly power, He had a strange way of showing it.

3) Jesus was a **lunatic**.

Well then, perhaps Jesus was just insane?

Consider the Sermon on the Mount in Matthew, chapters 5-7. Does this look to you like the ravings of a lunatic? Read again His deft answer to the people who wanted to catch Him in His words (Mark 12:13-17). Observe the brilliance and subtlety of His answer to those who wanted to stone the woman taken in adultery (John 8:1-11). This kind of savvy is hardly evidence of madness. No wonder people who tried to trick Him were "astonished by his answer [and] became silent" (Luke 20:26). His lucidity, sense of perspective, irony, and humor do not bespeak madness but great sanity. Nor does even His iron resolve to meet His fate look like madness. We never get the impression that He *desires* death; instead He believes Himself to be commanded by God the Father to overcome death by giving His life "as a ransom for many" (1 Timothy 2:6).

4) Jesus was a **light and fluffy New Ager.**

Well, yes, say some, Jesus *did* claim to be God. But He meant it in an Eastern or "New Age" way. He was merely asserting His "God consciousness" in an attempt to awaken this same consciousness in us. He was, in short, a guru to the Jewish people. When He says He is the Son of God, He means we are *all* children of God and, indeed, we are God ourselves if we but realize it.

It's an interesting thought, but it's not what Jesus said. On the contrary, He affirms that God is *Lord* of heaven and earth, not that He *is* heaven and earth. Indeed, He does not speak of God as identical with Creation; He speaks of Him in a thoroughly Jewish sense as Transcendent Creator, Judge and Father (Matthew 19:4; 6:14-15). He does not tell His disciples they are parts of God; He plainly reminds them they are sinners in need of salvation who are, apart from Him alone, incapable of accomplishing that salvation or anything else (John 15:5). Far from affirming that He's OK and We're OK, He frequently tells us we are evil, but He is without sin; we are from below, but He is from above (John 8:1-11; 8:23). He insists that the way to life is not by discovering our divinity but by putting our faith exclusively in Him.

Very well then, if the records are reliable they clearly show us a man who is neither merely nice, nor a liar, nor insane, nor a New Age guru. Yet He still stands before us implacably asking, "Who do you say I am?" (Matthew 16:15). And as He does so in an ever more insistent voice, we begin to feel the grip of C.S. Lewis' logic that

> ...the historical difficulty of giving for the life, sayings and influence of Jesus any explanation that is not harder than the Christian explanation is very great. The discrepancy between the depth and sanity and (let me add) shrewdness of his moral teaching and the rampant megalomania which must lie behind his theological teaching unless He is indeed God, has never been satisfactorily got over. (C.S. Lewis, *Miracles*)

Which leads us to only one conclusion:

5) Jesus is the **Lord**.

As we consider all the evidence, there is only one possibility that truly satisfies: Jesus is who He says He is. He is God in the flesh. He is the eternal Son of God, the Messiah, sent to save the world from its sins. He indeed is the Lord of the Universe, who came to give us eternal life. He really and truly shed His blood for us on the cross and He really and truly rose from the dead and ascended into heaven. Now He offers us all the riches of His love, mercy, forgiveness, joy, power and peace by the gift of the Holy Spirit, and eternal life with His Father through the sacraments of His Church, which is His body.

~

Please consider praying the following prayer as a next step. After praying this prayer, go to a Catholic church and pray in front of the tabernacle where the Eucharist is contained. Attend Mass, on both Sunday and, if possible, even daily. Contact your local Catholic parish and set up a meeting with a priest. He will offer you guidance on how you can progress in your spiritual life.

Prayer to Follow Jesus

Jesus, I believe You are God's only-begotten Son.

I believe that, as the Incarnate Son of God, You can lead me in a way that honors Your Father and teaches me to walk in Your Way as Your disciple.

I ask You to come into my heart and to guide me to the fullness of the riches of Your Spirit in the inheritance of your saints. I accept You as the Messiah and want to honor You as Lord. Help me to find You where You may be found, in Your Father's House, the temple which is the Church, the body of Christ. Help me to find the answers to the questions I still have, to pursue You in faith and trust, and to let nothing distract me from persevering in faith and obedience to You.

Please show me the way to true peace, love and happiness.

Amen.

PART 3
AND THE STORY CONTINUES

During the last years of His life, a band of followers traveled with Jesus as He made His way around Galilee and Judea, healing and teaching. From among these disciples He chose twelve as his *apostles* (meaning "those sent out"). From these leaders He further singled out one. Jesus changed his name from Simon to Peter, meaning "rock," and declared that upon this "rock" He would build His Church (see Matthew 16:18).

The apostles lived with Jesus for three years, heard His teaching, and witnessed His miracles. Yet when Jesus was arrested, all but one fled in fear. Even the "rock," Peter, denied Him.

Surprisingly, at first, Jesus' resurrection did not appear to change them much. The remaining eleven apostles dismissed the first reports as "idle tales" (see Luke 24: 11). The apostle Thomas refused to believe until he put his fingers in the wounds of the risen Christ.

But Jesus finally appeared to all of them and instructed them to tell the whole world about Him. First, though, they were to wait in Jerusalem for what Jesus called "the promise of the Father"(Acts 1:4). Nine days after Jesus' ascension into heaven, the apostles, Mary the mother of Jesus, and over a hundred others found out what Jesus meant. It was the Jewish Feast of Pentecost, and the power of the Holy Spirit filled them so profoundly that they would never be the same. Formerly fearful and faltering, they now became bold, joyful, and even exuberant. They burst out into the streets, crowded with pilgrims from every part of the known world.

The apostles stood up, and with Peter as their spokesman, fearlessly witnessed to the resurrection of Christ. Thousands heard their proclamation, each in his own native tongue, and three thousand, through the waters of baptism, entered into this new community of forgiveness, joy, and freedom. It was like a reverse of the tower of Babel (Genesis 11). The different languages, originally a sign of the division caused by sin, were now a sign that God was bringing the fragmented human family back together again.

This day, Pentecost, was truly the birthday of the Church and showed what Jesus' death and resurrection were really about. Salvation from sin means not just wiping the offenses off God's record book. Sin deeply wounds, binds, and weakens us, cutting the life-line between us and our divine power-source and breaking our relationships with other people. Jesus died to reconnect us with God, making possible an intimate relationship with Him as our loving Father. All those who love Him become our brothers and sisters. And the power of His merciful, healing love, which Scripture calls "grace," becomes available to us through the Holy Spirit to make us new men and women, all resembling our elder brother Jesus.

From its very birth, the Church has been *catholic* (from the Greek word meaning "universal" or "whole"). Though the word itself doesn't appear in the New Testament, the concept is everywhere. This new community founded on Peter, the Rock, is not some exotic cult, an exclusive club for saints. Rather, it is God's family where everybody is welcomed as a member, regardless of race or color, faults or failings. The Church, then, is a universal "hospital for sinners" where all can experience the healing, transforming grace of God, and become the people God intended them to be.

But the presence of God's grace did not mean that all were instantly made perfect. Some Christians continued to sin seriously, and others entered into serious disputes. It was the apostles, gathered around Peter, who settled these disputes and kept discipline in the family, maintaining its unity and integrity.

Peter and the apostles were also responsible for feeding the family (John 21:15-19), so that sinners could grow into saints. One way they did this was through passing on to the people the words and deeds of Jesus, including the story of His death and resurrection, and explaining to them the implications for their lifestyle.

Another way they did this was by presiding over the sacraments—the tangible ways that the disciples were touched by Jesus' life-changing grace. Baptism, Confirmation, Anointing of the Sick, Penance, Matrimony, and Holy Orders are all visible signs, instituted by Christ, through which the power of Pentecost can flow into our lives. The Eucharist, the remembrance of the Last Supper, has been the center of Christian life from its very earliest days. Through this breaking of the bread (Acts 2: 42), the apostles fed the Church with the Body of Christ, the bread of life (John 6:48-59). Through Holy Orders, the apostles ordained assistants (Acts 14:23) and later successors to continue the work of nourishing the family, keeping it together, and keeping it faithful to the "whole" (Catholic) truth. The apostles' successors came to be known as *episkopoi* ("overseers")—*bishops*, in English (Philippians 1:1). The bishop of Rome, where Peter died, had a special role as the successor of Peter. As father of the Christians in Rome and, in wider sense, in the whole world, he became known as the *papa* ("father") of the family—the pope.

Some of the truths about Jesus, as preached by the apostles, were eventually written by some of these same apostles and their followers. By the second century AD, these writings, collected and preserved by the Church, came to be recognized as having been inspired by the Holy Spirit. We now call them the New Testament. But these brief writings were never intended to convey all that the apostles learned from Jesus in the three years they lived with Him. Many truths were passed on by word of mouth, example, and lived experience, and are known as Sacred Tradition (2 Thessalonians 2:15).

So this community—led by the successors of Peter and the apostles—nourished by Scripture, Tradition, and the sacraments—grew and spread over the pagan Roman Empire and beyond. The brutal force of Roman tyranny could not stop Jesus' love; neither could it stop the spread of that love through His Church. After three hundred years of intermittent and bloody persecution, even the Roman emperor Constantine finally confessed Jesus as his Lord.

Over the course of the following centuries, disputes arose about what Jesus and the apostles really taught. According to the New Testament pattern (see Acts 15: 6-29), the successors of the apostles, in communion with the successor of Peter, repeatedly gathered in *ecumenical* (world-wide) councils to settle these questions decisively. Refusing to accept this apostolic authority, many groups broke away from the Catholic Church. They opted for a partial selection of truth (*heresy* comes from the Greek word for "choice") rather than faithfulness to the whole. The result has been a weakening of Christian witness, and a fragmentation reminiscent of Babel. We are not responsible for splits of the past. But it is our responsibility to witness together with an undivided voice to the fullness of His truth.

Fullness of truth. Fullness of life. Fullness of the means of grace. This is what *Catholic* means. This is what we need; indeed, what the world needs.

But what about the atrocities committed by Catholics in the Crusades, Renaissance Popes with illegitimate children, Catholic clergy guilty of sexual abuse? There is no need to try to deny the failings of various Church members and even leaders. The New Testament did not try to cover up Judas' betrayal or Peter's denial. After all, the Church is a hospital for sinners.

But isn't it remarkable that after 2,000 years of imperfect members being led by imperfect people, the Catholic Church not only survives but even thrives? At more than one billion members, it is the largest single religious group in the world. The grace of God has sustained the Church—and God has promised to do so until the end of time (see Matthew 28:20).

There is something even more remarkable than this. In every age there have been sinners who have entered this hospital and become saints through the transforming power of Pentecost—Peter, the coward-turned-Rock; Paul, the murderer-become-martyr; all the way to Mother Teresa of Calcutta, whose relentless love touched the very heart of the 20th century.

So what about you? Jesus came that you might have life, and have it abundantly (John 10:10). Why settle for anything less?

PART 4
QUO VADIS? (WHERE ARE YOU GOING?)

Legend has it that in later years St. Peter, the head of the apostles, who was by that time the first bishop of Rome, fled the city to escape the persecution of Christians taking place there. While on the road he met Jesus coming from the other direction. Peter asked Jesus, *"Quo vadis?* [Where are You going?]"

Jesus answered that He was going to Rome to die again for His people. Chastened, Peter immediately turned around and headed back to Rome.

Now we have arrived at a similar crossroads, a moment of decision or delay, action or inaction, where you must choose whether you will act on what you know to be true about Jesus. This choice is not some small matter, but one of great importance. The time is now to seriously consider and respond to His call—to follow Him.

What can you do to respond to what Jesus has done for you? Here are *three recommendations*:

1. **Purchase a Bible and begin reading the Gospels**.
    Remember, though, that while the Bible contains life-changing, eternal truth, it is not always an easy book to understand. St. Peter stated as much when he said that some can "twist [the Scriptures] to their own destruction" (2 Peter 3:16). So you need to be careful.

It's one thing to break a man-made law. It's far worse to get one of God's teachings wrong—that could have eternal consequences. We need to follow the lead of the Ethiopian eunuch, who realized that he needed a teacher when he said, "How can I [understand] unless someone guides me?" (Acts 8:31) This leads us to the next recommendation.

2.   If you are a non-Catholic, **find a local Catholic Church** and meet with a priest. The Catholic Church has been given the authority by Jesus to teach in His name. By following the Church that Jesus established, you can be sure that you are plugged into the apostolic faith—the faith that has been given the gifts of the sacraments, divinely-given leadership, and the promise of remaining faithful until the end of time.

While there are instances when individuals in the Church fall into error and sin, we need to realize that the Church is both divine and human. At no point, however, will the Church teach anything but the truth, because it is protected by the Holy Spirit. God has ordained that it will be here—with the Gospel fully intact—until the end of time.

If you are a former Catholic, meet with a priest to be reconciled with the Church through the sacrament of Penance. Confession, although a little scary to some, is liberating. Your confession is protected by the seal of confession, which means a priest can never reveal what he has heard. Quite simply, the confessional is the safest and best place on earth to ask God's forgiveness.

3. After a period of prayer, study, and frequenting the sacraments, **become active in your faith**. A believing Catholic is an *active* Catholic—through apostolic works and a life of prayer for the rest of the Church. Your new life of faith will be a fantastic journey. Be assured of the prayer support of your fellow members of the Church. Although you may never meet the humble priests, sisters, brothers, and lay Catholics dedicated to prayer, know that they are there praying for you.

Appendices

Appendix A

SORROWFUL MYSTERIES OF THE ROSARY

Meditation on these five mysteries of the Rosary is traditionally on Tuesday and Friday. These mysteries commemorate five of the key moments in the Passion of Jesus, starting with His profound suffering in the Garden of Gethsemane, continuing through two of the indignities He suffered during His trial before Pontius Pilate (the scourging and the crowning with thorns), His taking up the Cross, and ending with His crucifixion. These are the foundational events upon which our salvation is built; they show us in a most profound way that love—for it to be authentic—involves sacrifice. As Jesus Himself said, "Greater love has no man than this, that [he] lay down his life for his friends" (John 15:13).

For meditations on each of the five sorrowful mysteries, go to the Catholic Passion Outreach website www.evangelization.com

1. **The Agony in the Garden**
2. **The Scourging at the Pillar**
3. **The Crowning with Thorns**
4. **The Carrying of the Cross**
5. **The Crucifixion and Death of Our Lord**

Appendix B

STATIONS OF THE CROSS

One of the most popular and traditional Catholic devotions, the Stations of the Cross commemorates the fourteen key events in the Passion of Jesus. The Stations have been prayed in one form or another for at least 1,000 years. For meditations on each of the Stations, go to the Catholic Passion Outreach website www.evangelization.com

I.   **Jesus is Condemned to Death**

II.   **Jesus Takes Up His Cross**

III.   **Jesus Falls the First Time**

IV.   **Jesus Meets His Mother**

V.   **Simon Of Cyrene Helps Jesus Carry His Cross**

VI.   **Veronica Wipes The Face Of Jesus**

VII.   **Jesus Falls The Second Time**

VIII.   **Jesus Meets The Women Of Jerusalem**

IX.   **Jesus Falls The Third Time**

X.   **Jesus Is Stripped Of His Garments**

XI.   **Jesus Is Nailed To The Cross**

XII.   **Jesus Dies On The Cross**

XIII.   **Jesus Is Laid In The Arms Of His Blessed Mother**

XIV.   **Jesus Is Laid In The Tomb**

Appendix C

SEVEN LAST WORDS OF CHRIST

These seven "words" (or sayings) were spoken by Jesus during His agony on the cross. Each is rich in theological symbolism, springing forth from the depths of Christ's soul to give us profound insight into God's plan of salvation and His great love for us. So moving are these words of Jesus that they were set to music by several of the great composers (Haydn, Franck). Their transcendent power has inspired countless millions to greater faith in and reverence for the saving power of the Cross. For a more detailed account of this devotion, go to www.evangelization.com

1. **Father, forgive them; for they know not what they do** (Luke 23:34).
2. **Woman, behold your son! ... Behold your mother!** (John 19:26-27).
3. **I thirst** (John 19:28).
4. **This day you will be with me in Paradise** (Luke 23:43).
5. **My God, My God, why have You forsaken Me?** (Matthew 27:46; Mk 15:34).
6. **It is finished** (John 19:30).
7. **Father, into Your hands, I commend My spirit** (Luke 23:46).

Resources

The following materials can be found on the Internet using one of the search engines or at your local Catholic bookstore.

Adult Faith Formation Programs

Study group materials on *A Guide to the Passion: 100 Questions About The Passion of The Christ* (Ascension Press) can be found at www.evangelization.com. They include a Small Group Handbook, a Leader's Manual, and free promotional materials for your diocese, parish, or group. These study materials will help you run an excellent Lenten program, and are also appropriate for use throughout the year.

Bible Study Programs

- *Catholic Scripture Study* by Jeff Cavins, Scott Hahn, and Mark Shea (Catholic Exchange)
- *The Great Adventure Bible Timeline* by Jeff Cavins, Tim Gray, and Sarah Christmyer (Ascension Press)

Books/Articles/Audios/Videos

Unless otherwise indicated, all of the following materials are books.

Catholic Teaching and Practice

For Adults:
- *Bible Basics* by Steve Kellmeyer
- *Exploring the Catholic Church* by Marcellino D'Ambrosio, Ph.D.
- *Fundamentals of the Faith* by Peter Kreeft
- *Handbook of Christian Apologetics* by Peter Kreeft & Ronald Tacelli
- *Making Senses Out of Scripture: Reading the Bible as the First Christians Did* by Mark P. Shea
- *Miracles* by C.S. Lewis
- *The Belief of Catholics* by Ronald Knox
- *The Catechism of the Catholic Church* (second edition)
- *The Everlasting Man* by G.K. Chesterton
- *The Life of Christ* by Fulton J. Sheen
- *The Spirit of Catholicism* by Karl Adam
- *Theology for Beginners* by Frank Sheed

- *Theology and Sanity* by Frank Sheed
- *Welcome Home* – Romero, Cleaveau, et al.
- *What Catholics Really Believe* by Karl Keating
- *Why Be Catholic?* (audio) by Marcellino D'Ambrosio, Ph.D.

For Teenagers:
- *Ask the Bible Geek* by Mark Hart
- *Did Adam & Eve Have Belly Buttons?* by Matthew Pinto
- *Father McBride's Teen Catechism* by Fr. Alfred McBride
- *Prove It!* Series by Amy Welborn

For non-Catholic Christians:
- *Born Fundamentalist, Born Again Catholic* by David Currie
- *By What Authority? An Evangelical Discovers Catholic Tradition* by Mark P. Shea
- *Catholic and Christian* by Alan Schreck
- *My Life on the Rock* by Jeff Cavins
- *Rome Sweet Home* by Scott and Kimberly Hahn
- *Surprised by Truth* by Patrick Madrid
- *This is My Body: An Evangelical Discovers the Real Presence* by Mark P. Shea
- *Why Do Catholics Genuflect?* by Al Kresta

The Crucifixion and the Passion

- *Crucifixion* by Martin Hengel
- *His Cross in Your Life* by Fr. Bertrand Weaver
- *Life is Worth Living* (video) by Fulton Sheen
- *The Agony of Jesus* by Padre Pio of Pietrelcina
- *The Day Christ Died* by Jim Bishop
- *The Passion: Reflections on the Suffering and Death of Jesus* by Paul Thigpen
- *The Passion of Jesus and Its Hidden Meaning* by Fr. James Groenings
- *The Robe* by Lloyd C. Douglas
- *The Spear* by Louis de Wohl
- *The Way of the Cross* by Caryll Houselander
- *What Jesus Saw from the Cross* by A.G. Sertillanges
- *When They Crucified My Lord* by Brother Ramon

Private Revelations related to the Passion

Note: Although the Catholic Church accepts many private revelations, readers should always proceed with caution—private revelations are not part of the official deposit of Catholic teaching and may contain theological errors. Before reading materials containing private revelations, first read the books *A Still Small Voice* by Fr. Benedict Groeschel, *The Rapture Trap* by Paul Thigpen, and *The Passion: Reflections on the Suffering and Death of Jesus* by Paul Thigpen.

Books used as resources for the film:
- *The Dolorous Passion of Our Lord Jesus Christ* by Ven. Anne Catherine Emmerich
- *The Mystical City of God, The Divine History of the Virgin Mother of God* by Ven. Maria de Agreda

Other books that discuss the Passion:
- *The Life and Revelations of Anne Catherine Emmerich* by Rev. Carl E. Schmoeger
- *Revelations of St. Bridget on the Life and Passion of Our Lord and the Life of His Blessed Mother* by St. Bridget of Sweden
- *The Holy Shroud and Four Visions* by Rev. Patrick O'Connell and Rev. C.M. Carty

Shroud of Turin

- *A Doctor at Calvary* by Pierre Barbet
- *Report on the Shroud of Turin* by John Heller

Suffering

- *Amazing Grace for Those Who Suffer* by Jeff Cavins and Matthew Pinto
- *Does Suffering Make Sense?* by Russell Shaw
- *Lessons from the School of Suffering* by Rev. Jim Willig with Tammy Bundy
- *Salvifici Doloris,* encyclical letter of Pope John Paul II on suffering
- *The School of Jesus Crucified (The Lessons of Calvary in Daily Catholic Life)* by Fr. Ignatius, Passionist.
- *The Way of the Cross* by Pope John Paul II
- *They Bore the Wounds of Christ: The Mystery of the Sacred Stigmata* by Michael Freze
- *Turning Pain into Gain: Understanding the Mystery of Suffering* (audio) by Jeff Cavins
- *Why Must I Suffer?* by Fr. F.J. Remler

Internet Resources

Catholic Faith – General
- www.ascensionpress.com – site of Ascension Press
- www.thebibletimeline.com – *The Great Adventure* Bible Seminar site
- www.catholicexchange.com – *the* Catholic homepage on the Web
- www.catholicscripturestudy.com – Catholic Scripture Study website
- www.crossroadsinitiative.com – a Catholic education and evangelization apostolate

- www.evangelization.com – Catholic Passion Outreach site; free study materials on *The Passion of The Christ*
- www.luminousmedia.org– Catholic audio and video materials; division of Ascension Press
- www.theologyofthebody.com – Information on the Theology of the Body
- www.usccb.org – the site of the U.S. Catholic Bishops
- www.vatican.va – the official site of the Holy See

Shroud of Turin
- www.shroud.com
- www.shroud.org

Finding a Catholic Church
- www.masstimes.org – provides a comprehensive listing of every Catholic parish in North America

Broadcast Media

- Eternal Word Television Network - www.ewtn.com
- Relevant Radio (Starboard Network) - www.relevantradio.com

Additional resources are available on the
Catholic Passion Outreach website www.evangelization.com

Acknowledgments

The following authors contributed to this book:

Tom Allen serves as editor-in-chief and publisher of *CatholicExchange.com*, a popular daily Internet portal. He is founder and president of the American Family Film Foundation and a producer for the Starboard/Relevant Radio network. Tom worked on the marketing and distribution of *The Passion of The Christ*.

Marcellino D'Ambrosio, Ph.D. earned his doctorate in historical theology from the Catholic University of America under the direction of Avery Cardinal Dulles. After eight years teaching at Loyola College and the University of Dallas, he left academia to direct the *CrossroadsInitiative.com*, a Catholic apostolate of evangelization and renewal.

Matthew Pinto is the founder and president of Ascension Press, a co-founder of *CatholicExchange.com* and *Envoy* magazine, and the author of the best-selling question-and-answer book *Did Adam & Eve Have Belly-Buttons?* With Jeff Cavins, he serves as co-editor of the *Amazing Grace* Series of books.

Mark Shea is a popular Catholic writer and speaker, and serves as senior content editor for *CatholicExchange.com* and co-author (with Dr. Scott Hahn) of the Catholic Scripture Study available at that site. He is the author of *Making Senses Out of Scripture: Reading the Bible as the First Christians Did* and *This is My Body: An Evangelical Discovers the Real Presence*.

Paul Thigpen, Ph.D. edits *The Catholic Answer* magazine and has written thirty best-selling books, including *The Passion: Reflections on the Suffering and Death of Jesus Christ*. He is also the founder and executive director of the Stella Maris Center for Faith and Culture in Savannah, Georgia.

Editorial and technical assistance by Annamarie Adkins, Sue Allen, Anthony DeBellis, Michael Flickinger, Michael Fontecchio, Joseph Lewis, Michael J. Miller, and Lucy Scholand. Marketing and public relations coordinated by Tara Williams.

CATHOLIC PASSION OUTREACH

—www.evangelization.com—

*T*he *Passion of The Christ* is an epic movie masterpiece that is going to change countless lives. It is not just another extraordinary Hollywood production—it's a call for each of us to encounter the person of Jesus Christ.

The Passion of The Christ offers an unprecedented cultural opportunity for you to spread, strengthen, and share the Catholic faith with your family and friends. Unlike any other, *this movie will inspire hearts and change minds. And it will evoke questions.*

You can play a role in bringing home this film's inspiring message. Catholic Passion Outreach has prepared some great resources to help you in your evangelization efforts. Go to www.evangelization.com to download our free outreach resources, including the *Small Group Handbook, Leader's Manual,* and *Diocese/Parish Action Plan.* Full-color and black and white posters and flyers are also available, and you can order additional copies of *A Guide to the Passion* for your parish, family, and friends.

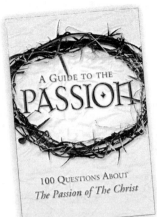

100 QUESTIONS ABOUT
The Passion of The Christ

A GUIDE
TO THE
PASSION

Bulk Discounts
Available

A Guide to the Passion retails for $5.95, but you can purchase it in bulk for less than $1.

# of copies	*Price Each*	*Your Discount*	*Total*
2	$5	16%	$10
5	$4.50	24%	$22.50
10	$4	33%	$40
25	$3.50	41%	$87.50
50	$2.50	58%	$125
100	$1.95	67%	$195
250	$1.30	78%	$325
500	$1.15	81%	$575
1,000	$1	83%	$1,000
2,000	$0.90	85%	$1,800

Call **888-488-6789** for details or order online at www.evangelization.com

100% of the royalties from this book will be donated to the promotion of the film and other evangelization programs.

- - - - - - - - - - - - - - - - - - -

❏ Yes, please send me copies of *A Guide to the Passion*

Send me _____ booklets x _____ea   =$_____

Shipping   =$_____

Extra Donation for Your Apostolate   =$_____

Total   =$_____

❏ Cash   ❏ Check   ❏ Credit Card

Priority S/H Rates:
2-5 copies $4.60
6-9 copies $7.50
10+ copies . . . . . . UPS Shipping

Call us for additional shipping rate information

Please make checks payable to: Catholic Exchange
P.O. Box 231820 Encinitas, CA 92023
Tel: 888-477-1982 E-mail: tkyd@catholicexchange.com

Bill to Name_____

Address_____

City_____State____Zip_____

Phone_____Fax_____

E-mail_____

Card #: _____

MC ❏   Visa ❏   Discover ❏   Exp. Date:_____
                                              (required!)
Ship to Name_____

Address_____

City_____State____Zip_____

Phone_____Fax_____

Life is Short.
Support Good Media.

The **American Family Film Foundation (AFFF)** was founded to address the problem of the erosive influence of the media on youth and families. AFFF is a unique non-profit organization dedicated to the development and support of popular entertainment that is positive and enlightening.

We accomplish this goal by offering media that communicates our positive message. The Foundation serves as collaborator or producer on media projects that communicate our special niche. AFFF directly or indirectly helps realize projects of all sizes and ambitions – from websites to 30-second spots to video programs to full-length feature films. We also offer media consultation and production assistance to non-profits looking to effectively communicate their messages.

AFFF's team of professionals work in development, production, post-production, promotion and the business side of the media industry. Our expertise enables us to create high-quality productions at a significantly reduced cost for distribution to schools, families, social service organizations, and community groups throughout the country.

We rely on your support to help us accomplish our mission. Please make a tax-deductible donation to us online at www.afff.tv or mail your tax-deductible donation to us at:

AFFF
PO Box 231664
Encinitas, CA 92023

Thank you.

www.afff.tv